EMPOWERING WOMEN

EMPOWERING WOMEN

India's Reservation Triumph

MACK RAFEAL

Spectra Enterprise

CONTENTS

Table of Content

3.1 Grassroots movements for women's rights

3.2 Activists and organizations leading the charge

3.3 Challenges faced in pushing for legislation

Chapter 4: The Controversy Surrounding Women's Reservation

4.1 Opposition and criticisms

1. Misconceptions and myths

2. Political and cultural resistance

4.2 Debates within feminist circles

Intersectionality and inclusivity

Chapter 5: Legislative Progress and Setbacks

5.1 Legislative history of the Women's Reservation Bill

5.2 Attempts to pass the bill

5.3 Challenges and setbacks faced in the legislative process

Chapter 6: Success Stories from Reservations

6.1 Women who benefited from reservations

6.2 Political success stories

6.3 Economic and social impact on reserved constituencies

Chapter 7: Overcoming Challenges in Implementation

7.1 Addressing reservations' limitations

7.2 Ensuring effective implementation

7.3 Evaluating and refining policies based on feedback

Chapter 8: The Ripple Effect on Society

8.1 Changing societal attitudes towards women in leadership

8.2 Impact on gender roles and stereotypes

8.3 The role of education and awareness

Chapter 9: Looking Ahead - Future Possibilities and Challenges

9.1 Potential improvements and expansions

9.2 Policy recommendations

9.3 Addressing emerging challenges and adapting to societal changes

Introduction

In the perplexing embroidery of India's socio-political scene, the strengthening of ladies has arisen as an essential concern, mirroring the country's obligation to inclusivity and orientation fairness. Among the multi-layered procedures utilized to address this objective, the booking framework has collected huge consideration. India's Booking Win in enabling ladies connotes an extraordinary change in the political worldview, meaning to destroy conventional boundaries that have long frustrated ladies' dynamic support in administration. This drive mirrors a nuanced comprehension of the difficulties looked by ladies and endeavors to make a more impartial society by giving them a significant stake in dynamic cycles.

Authentic Setting

To grasp the meaning of India's Booking Win, one should dig into the authentic setting that molded the story of ladies' political interest. India, notwithstanding its rich social variety, has wrestled with profoundly instilled male centric standards that consigned ladies to the peripheries of public life. The battle for orientation equity picked up speed with the coming of the women's activist development during the twentieth hundred years, inciting a reconsideration of cultural standards and practices. In any case, the political circle remained generally male-overwhelmed, hindering the interpretation of these yearnings into substantial additions for ladies.

The Beginning of Reservation Strategy

The beginning of India's Booking Win can be followed back to the acknowledgment that aloof measures were inadequate to change the verifiable awkwardness. The composers of the Indian Constitution, mindful of the requirement for governmental policy regarding minorities in society, presented arrangements that considered the booking of seats in administrative bodies for underestimated gatherings, including ladies. The booking strategy was at first executed for Planned Standings (SCs) and Booked Clans (STs) to address authentic treacheries and guarantee their portrayal in political establishments. Over the long run, the acknowledgment of the exceptional difficulties looked by ladies incited a change in perspective, prompting the expansion of reservations to incorporate ladies at different degrees of administration.

Challenges Looked by Ladies in Legislative issues

Before the approach of the booking strategy, ladies confronted diverse difficulties that hindered their political interest. Well established cultural standards, combined with financial variations and absence of admittance to schooling, delivered a huge piece of the female populace politically minimized. In addition, the pervasiveness of orientation based viciousness and separation further deterred ladies from entering the political field. India's Booking Win looked to destroy these boundaries by giving an organized structure that recognized the verifiable disappointment of ladies as well as effectively pursued their mix into the political standard.

Effect of Reservation on Ladies' Portrayal

The booking strategy's effect on ladies' portrayal in regulative bodies has been significant, introducing another period of inclusivity. Saved seats for ladies at the nearby, state, and public levels have empowered a different companion of ladies to partake in dynamic cycles. This has not just moved assumptions about ladies' capacity to oversee however has likewise filled in as an impetus for change inside networks. The presence of ladies in administrative roles has prompted the prioritization of issues influencing ladies, kids, and underestimated networks, carrying a more all encompassing point of view to strategy definition.

Engaging Grassroots Initiative

One of the remarkable accomplishments of India's Booking Win is the strengthening of grassroots initiative. The booking strategy, especially at the Panchayat (nearby administration) level, has seen a flood in ladies pioneers. These grassroots delegates, frequently hailing from impeded foundations, carry a novel point of view to administration, grounded in their lived encounters. This has democratized the political interaction as well as made ready for local area driven improvement drives that address the particular requirements of the most weak fragments of society.

Difficulties and Reactions

While India's Booking Win has taken huge steps in upgrading ladies' political support, it has not been without its portion of difficulties and reactions. Some contend that the booking strategy, by assigning a specific level of seats for ladies, may unintentionally propagate the thought of hypocrisy, subverting the meritocratic standards of a majority rules government. Also, concerns have been raised about the nature of administration, with doubters addressing whether the booking strategy has converted into viable approach execution and significant cultural change.

Catalyzing Social Movements

Past the mathematical portrayal, India's Booking Win has catalyzed social movements by testing winning generalizations and standards. The perceivability of ladies in influential positions has tested profoundly dug in orientation predispositions, motivating an age of little kids to seek to influential places. This social change isn't restricted to metropolitan focuses however has permeated into country scenes, testing

One of the inconspicuous yet significant results of India's Booking Win is the catalyzation of social movements. The perceivability of ladies in positions of authority challenges cliché ideas about ladies' abilities and jobs. As ladies demonstrate their backbone in administration, generalizations that once bound them to conventional jobs are step by step disintegrating. The booking strategy has turned into an impetus for destroying orientation predispositions and moving an age of little kids to seek to administrative roles, both in governmental issues and different circles.

The Way Forward

As India's Booking Win keeps on advancing, it is vital to evaluate the way forward for supported progress. Endeavors should be made to address the difficulties related with posturing and guarantee that saved seats convert into significant political office for ladies. Upgrading the nature of portrayal requires a far reaching approach, incorporating instruction, expertise building, and backing structures for ladies pioneers.

Besides, encouraging a climate that advances orientation inclusivity in all parts of society is central. Regulative bodies ought to act as reference points of variety, mirroring the pluralistic idea of Indian culture. Continuous drives, for example, mindfulness missions and limit building programs, can assume a significant part in testing generalizations and cultivating an ethos of correspondence.

1. **Historical context of gender inequality in India**

   The verifiable setting of orientation imbalance in India is a mind boggling story profoundly laced with the nation's social, social, and monetary development. The foundations of orientation abberations stretch back hundreds of years, formed by customary standards, strict principles, and financial designs that allocated ladies subordinate jobs in both private and open arenas. To comprehend the moves ladies confronted and keep on confronting, one should dive into the perplexing layers of India's verifiable woven artwork.

   Antiquated India saw the rise of assorted civic establishments, each adding to the forming of cultural standards and orientation jobs. While antiquated Indian texts, for example, the Vedas and Upanishads displayed occasions of ladies participating in scholarly and profound pursuits, the truth was in many cases more nuanced. The standing framework, a characterizing component of old Indian culture, delineated networks, consigning specific gatherings, including ladies, to subordinate positions.

   The idea of patriliny, where familial ancestry and legacy went through male relatives, built up the power of men in the social request. This male centric design showed itself in different parts of day to day existence, from legacy regulations to marriage customs, sustaining orientation pecking orders. Ladies' admittance to instruction was much of the time restricted, and their jobs were bound to home-grown spaces, answerable for the prosperity of the family and the propagation of social and familial practices.

   The appearance of different traditions and domains in middle age India further molded orientation elements. While certain rulers were known for advancing orientation inclusivity, others built up conventional standards that restricted ladies' office. The act of purdah (veiling and detachment of ladies) acquired conspicuousness in specific locales, confining ladies' perceivability openly spaces and supporting thoughts of unobtrusiveness and prudence.

Imperialism denoted a critical defining moment in India's set of experiences, acquainting new elements with orientation relations. The English frontier organization, while achieving certain financial changes, frequently supported existing man centric designs. The presentation of English schooling and legitimate changes, while adding to the rise of a cutting edge working class, had shifted suggestions for ladies across various social layers.

For world class ladies in metropolitan places, openness to Western thoughts of women's liberation and individual freedoms energized goals for balance. Be that as it may, for ladies in provincial regions and minimized networks, the effect was not as uniform. The pioneer organization's comprehension and understanding of nearby traditions in some cases prompted the burden of specific standards, worsening existing orientation disparities.

The battle for India's freedom in the twentieth century saw the dynamic cooperation of ladies in the public development. Figures like Sarojini Naidu, Kamala Nehru, and Annie Besant assumed vital parts, featuring the capability of ladies as influencers. In any case, the post-autonomy time frame brought to the front the tirelessness of profoundly imbued orientation predispositions.

The drafting of the Indian Constitution in 1950 denoted a huge second, with the designers perceiving the need to address orientation differences. Central freedoms and standards of fairness were revered, establishing the groundwork for a more comprehensive society. However, the difficulties persevered as sociosocial standards kept on molding discernments and works on, restraining the full acknowledgment of ladies' privileges.

The 1970s saw the development of the women's activist development in India, resembling worldwide endeavors for orientation equity. The development meant to challenge unfair regulations, rehearses, and cultural standards, pushing for ladies' independence and equivalent open doors. The Council on the Situation with Ladies in India, led by Vina Mazumdar, assumed an essential part in molding suggestions that would ultimately add to governmental policy regarding minorities in society measures, remembering bookings for people for official bodies.

Notwithstanding these endeavors, the 1980s and 1990s saw continuous battles against orientation based savagery, segregation, and abberations in training and work. The perseverance of practices like female child murder, settlement related brutality, and inconsistent admittance to assets highlighted the well established nature of orientation disparity.

The turn of the 21st century denoted a recharged obligation to tending to orientation variations, both officially and socially. Legitimate changes, like revisions to hostile to assault regulations and the presentation of regulation against aggressive behavior at home, flagged a developing acknowledgment of the requirement for exhaustive measures. Nonetheless, the execution of these regulations and their viability in testing dug in standards stays a work underway.

In this verifiable setting, the booking strategy for ladies in India's political circle arose as an essential mediation. The comprehension that uninvolved measures were lacking to address the authentic irregularity prompted the acknowledgment that proactive advances were expected to politically inspire ladies. The booking strategy, at first executed for Planned Stations (SCs) and Planned Clans (STs), was stretched out to incorporate ladies, recognizing their exceptional difficulties and the requirement for portrayal at different degrees of administration.

India's Booking Win in engaging ladies through reservations mirrors a nuanced comprehension of the verifiable setting of orientation imbalance. It implies a takeoff from the inactivity of customary standards and a purposeful work to make a more comprehensive political scene. The strategy isn't simply a mathematical cure; it is a cognizant work to rework the story of ladies' support in administration, testing verifiable treacheries and encouraging a more fair society. As India wrestles with the intricacies of the 21st hundred years, the authentic setting of orientation disparity stays a vital piece of the continuous talk. The Booking Win, while a critical achievement, is only one part in the more extensive story of India's excursion towards orientation fairness. The diversity of orientation with position, class, and other social aspects requires far reaching and nuanced ways to deal with address the complex difficulties looked by ladies in India. The verifiable setting fills in as a guidepost, helping us to remember the unpredictable strings that have molded the texture of orientation relations and the basic to disentangle, question, and reproduce for a more evenhanded future.

2. **Need for affirmative action to empower women**

Chasing orientation correspondence, governmental policy regarding minorities in society has arisen as a basic device to review verifiable lopsided characteristics and enable ladies. This proactive methodology recognizes the foundational separation and settled in predispositions that have restricted ladies' chances in different circles of life. From instructive foundations to the work environment and political fields, governmental policy regarding minorities in society looks to make a more level battleground, perceiving that uninvolved measures alone may not be adequate to destroy profoundly imbued orientation variations. In this specific circumstance, looking at the requirement for governmental policy regarding minorities in society becomes basic to figure out its part in encouraging a more comprehensive and fair society.

Authentic Shameful acts and Determined Variations:

Governmental policy regarding minorities in society for ladies is established in the authentic shameful acts that have molded orientation elements over hundreds of years. Conventional standards, male centric designs, and biased rehearses consigned ladies to subordinate jobs, restricting their admittance to training, financial open doors, and dynamic cycles.

These verifiable treacheries cast a long shadow, appearing in determined differences that keep on blocking ladies' advancement. Governmental policy regarding minorities in society fills in as a component to address these verifiable uneven characters, giving ladies the resources to conquer foundational hindrances and take part more effectively in all features of society.

Schooling as an Establishment:

One of the essential regions where governmental policy regarding minorities in society assumes a vital part is in training. By and large, young ladies and ladies confronted hindrances to getting to quality instruction, sustaining a pattern of burden. Governmental policy regarding minorities in society measures, like grants, saved situates, and designated instructive projects, plan to overcome this issue. By guaranteeing more prominent portrayal of ladies in instructive foundations, governmental policy regarding minorities in society tends to quick variations as well as affects ladies' strengthening across different spaces. An informed lady is better prepared to explore cultural difficulties, add to financial turn of events, and partake definitively in city and political life.

Breaking the Unreasonable impediment in the Work environment:

The work environment has been a landmark for orientation uniformity, with ladies frequently confronting hindrances in professional success and equivalent compensation. Governmental policy regarding minorities in society as orientation standards, mentorship projects, and arrangements advancing balance between serious and fun activities looks to break the unreasonable impediment. By advancing the consideration of ladies in influential positions and dynamic positions, governmental policy regarding minorities in society challenges assumptions about ladies' capacities and encourages a more different and imaginative workplace. Organizations and associations that embrace governmental policy regarding minorities in society frequently experience improved efficiency, imagination, and a more comprehensive corporate culture.

Political Strengthening through Reservations:

Political portrayal is a vital part of strengthening, and governmental policy regarding minorities in society as reservations plays had an extraordinary impact. In nations like India, the booking of seats for ladies in regulative bodies has expanded their mathematical portrayal, giving a stage to voice their interests and shape strategies. This purposeful consideration recognizes the exceptional difficulties looked by ladies in governmental issues, from orientation based segregation to social predispositions. Governmental policy regarding minorities in society in legislative issues improves ladies' portrayal as well as carries different viewpoints to the very front, prompting more comprehensive and responsive administration.

Testing Generalizations and Evolving Insights:

Governmental policy regarding minorities in society fills in as an impetus for testing generalizations and changing cultural discernments about ladies' jobs and capacities.

By effectively advancing the consideration of ladies in generally male-overwhelmed fields, like science, innovation, designing, and arithmetic (STEM), governmental policy regarding minorities in society destroys generalizations that sustain orientation based segregation. Openness to different good examples and examples of overcoming adversity further dissolves imbued predispositions, empowering little kids and ladies to seek after goals past cultural assumptions. Along these lines, governmental policy regarding minorities in society turns into a system for social change, making ready for a more populist society.

Financial Effect and Neediness Mitigation:

Engaging ladies through governmental policy regarding minorities in society has sweeping monetary ramifications. Ladies' financial support adds to family pay as well as assumes a fundamental part in destitution easing. Governmental policy regarding minorities in society measures, for example, microfinance projects and business venture support, enable ladies to break liberated from patterns of neediness. Financial freedom upgrades ladies' dynamic independence, admittance to medical services and training, and generally prosperity. As ladies become monetary partners, the advantages reach out to families, networks, and the more extensive economy.

Diversity and Comprehensive Methodologies:

Governmental policy regarding minorities in society perceives the diversity of orientation with other social aspects, like position, race, identity, and sexual direction. Comprehensive methodologies that consider the interesting difficulties looked by underestimated and underrepresented gatherings of ladies guarantee that governmental policy regarding minorities in society is exhaustive and compelling. For instance, strategies that address the particular necessities of Dalit ladies, native ladies, or LGBTQ+ ladies perceive the different encounters inside the more extensive class of 'ladies.' Governmental policy regarding minorities in society, when executed with a multifaceted focal point, turns into a device for destroying numerous layers of segregation.

Legitimate Systems and Worldwide Responsibilities:

Governmental policy regarding minorities in society lines up with global responsibilities to advance orientation uniformity and ladies' strengthening. Different worldwide shows and arrangements underline the significance of governmental policy regarding minorities in society measures to address foundational orientation differences. Nations that embrace governmental policy regarding minorities in society exhibit their obligation to satisfying these commitments and establishing a climate where ladies' privileges are safeguarded and progressed. Legitimate systems that order orientation amounts, against segregation regulations, and measures to guarantee pay value add to the standardization of governmental policy regarding minorities in society standards.

Tending to the Parenthood Punishment:

One of the determined difficulties ladies face in the work environment is the parenthood punishment. Governmental policy regarding minorities in society estimates that give maternity leave, adaptable working plans, and backing for childcare assist with relieving the profession misfortunes frequently experienced by ladies subsequent to becoming moms. By perceiving and tending to the particular difficulties looked by ladies during their conceptive years, governmental policy regarding minorities in society turns into a device for holding and advancing ladies in the labor force, adding to a more adjusted and impartial expert scene.

Difficulties and Reactions:

While the requirement for governmental policy regarding minorities in society is clear, it isn't without difficulties and reactions. A contend that governmental policy regarding minorities in society might prompt hypocrisy, where people are incorporated simply to meet standards without resolving hidden fundamental issues. Also, worries about invert segregation have been raised, with pundits addressing whether governmental policy regarding minorities in society may unintentionally weakness certain gatherings. These difficulties feature the significance of nuanced and very much planned governmental policy regarding minorities in society arrangements that address explicit authentic and foundational disparities.

B. Purpose of the book

The reason for any book is a directing guide, a compass that coordinates the writer's expectations, and illuminates the peruser about the excursion they are going to embrace. Whether the work is fiction or genuine, scholastic or story, the reason shapes the substance, the tone, and the basic message. In investigating the reason for a book, one can unwind the writer's goals, the subjects they wish to convey, and the effect they desire to have on the perusers.

Illuminating and Illuminating:

Many books are made with the main role of edifying and illuminating their perusers. These could be scholarly texts, true to life works, or verifiable records that look to share information, bits of knowledge, and viewpoints on a specific subject. The writer plans to add to the aggregate comprehension of the point within reach, introducing realities, investigations, and understandings that draw in the peruser's keenness and interest. In this specific circumstance, the object is to go about as a wellspring of schooling and edification, encouraging a more profound perception of the topic.

Engaging and Getting away:

Fictitious works frequently have the reason for engaging and giving a getaway to perusers. Books, brief tales, and sorts like sci-fi or dream transport perusers to various universes, offering a break from the real world.

Through convincing stories, characters, and plots, these books mean to enamor the creative mind, inspire feelings, and give a type of amusement that goes past simple redirection. The reason here is to make a vivid encounter, permitting perusers to step into elective real factors and live vicariously through the characters for a brief time.

Rousing and Inspiring:

Self improvement guides, personal histories, and inspirational writing fill a need of rousing and persuading perusers. These works frequently draw from individual encounters, offering experiences, techniques, and life illustrations that can engage people to beat difficulties, put forth objectives, and seek after self-awareness. The motivation behind such books isn't just to share stories yet in addition to light a feeling of direction and assurance in the peruser, empowering them to explore life's excursion with strength and good faith.

Upholding and Affecting Change:

Certain books are driven by a reason to advocate for social or political change. These might be works of activism, declarations, or enticing stories that look to impact popular assessment and spike activity. Writers in this class utilize their words to feature shameful acts, champion causes, and motivate perusers to take part in developments that advance fairness, equity, or natural supportability. The object is to be an impetus for change, to incite thought, and to prepare people towards a typical reason.

Safeguarding and Reporting:

Authentic records, journals, and memoirs frequently fill the need of safeguarding and archiving occasions, encounters, or people for any kind of family down the line. By chronicling stories and points of view, these books add to the aggregate memory of social orders, guaranteeing that significant accounts are not lost to time. The reason here is chronicled, planning to report and safeguard the subtleties of human encounters, societies, and authentic ages.

Addressing and Testing Suspicions:

Certain works have the reason for addressing cultural standards, testing suppositions, and cultivating decisive reasoning. These books dig into the intricacies of human way of behaving, cultural designs, or philosophical requests. By empowering perusers to scrutinize their biases and contemplate elective viewpoints, the design is to invigorate scholarly interest and advance a more profound comprehension of the intricacies that shape our reality.

Hoisting the Tasteful Experience:

In writing and human expression, there is a reason to raise the tasteful experience. Verse, composition, and works of fiction frequently focus on language, style, and imaginative articulation. The reason here isn't exclusively utilitarian but instead to summon feelings, invigorate the faculties, and deal perusers an encounter that rises above the everyday. Such books intend to make excellence through language, having a permanent impact on the peruser's sensibilities.

Fundamentally, the reason for a book is pretty much as different as the class and subjects it can incorporate. Whether expecting to illuminate, engage, rouse, advocate, safeguard, question, or hoist, the writer's motivation shapes the peruser's commitment and the book's getting through influence. This reason reinvigorates the words on the page, producing an association between the writer and the peruser, and welcoming them to set out on a common excursion of investigation and revelation.

1. **Advocating for women's reservation in India**

   In the multifaceted scene of Indian governmental issues, the subject of orientation portrayal has been a persevering test. Perceiving the verifiable disappointment of ladies and the requirement for a more fair political field, there has been a developing promotion for ladies' booking in regulative bodies. The call for governmental policy regarding minorities in society through saved seats for ladies means to address the fundamental hindrances that have blocked ladies' support in administration. Advocates contend that such reservations are not just an issue of mathematical portrayal but rather an essential push toward destroying profoundly instilled orientation inclinations and encouraging a more comprehensive majority rules system.

   Verifiable Setting of Ladies' Political Support:

   The verifiable setting of ladies' political support in India uncovers a scene overwhelmed by male centric standards and settled in orientation differences. While ladies have been fundamental to social developments and assumed crucial parts in India's battle for freedom, their portrayal in formal political designs has been tragically lacking. The post-autonomy time saw some advancement, with prominent ladies pioneers arising on the political stage. Notwithstanding, the general portrayal of ladies in authoritative bodies has lingered behind, reflecting getting through cultural standards that have frustrated ladies from effectively taking part in administration.

   The Case for Ladies' Booking:

   Advocates for ladies' booking contend that such measures are a need to break the unfair limitation and rock the boat. India's Booking Win, at first tending to the verifiable treacheries looked by Planned Ranks (SCs) and Planned Clans (STs), was subsequently stretched out to incorporate ladies. The reasoning is established in the comprehension that aloof measures alone are deficient to address the well established predispositions that impede ladies' political cooperation. Held seats give an organized system to guarantee ladies' entrance into official bodies, making a pathway for their voices to be heard and viewpoints considered in strategy making.

   Upgrading A majority rule government and Inclusivity:

   One of the essential contentions for ladies' booking is upgrading the vote based texture of the nation potential. A majority rules system flourishes with different portrayal, mirroring the majority of voices inside society.

   Ladies, comprising a portion of the populace, offer extraordinary points of view and needs of real value. The shortfall of sufficient female portrayal subverts the standards of comprehensive administration, barring fundamental perspectives that are critical for tending to the complex difficulties looked by society.

   Groundbreaking Effect on Approaches:

   Saved seats for ladies groundbreakingly affect approaches and authoritative plans. Ladies pioneers, when furnished with a stage, have been instrumental in pushing for issues that straightforwardly influence ladies, kids, and under-estimated networks. From medical care to instruction and social government assistance, ladies' portrayal has prompted a more extensive and nuanced way to deal with strategy detailing. Advocates battle that a minimum amount of ladies in regulative bodies is fundamental for molding regulations and strategies that reverberate with the different recuirements of the populace.

Enabling Grassroots Initiative:

Ladies' booking isn't bound to public governmental issues yet stretches out to the grassroots level through Panchayati Raj establishments. This has engaged ladies at the nearby administration level, empowering them to effectively take part in dynamic cycles that influence their networks. Grassroots initiative by ladies has demonstrated to be an impetus for local area driven improvement drives, resolving issues like medical services, disinfection, and instruction that frequently lopsidedly influence ladies and underestimated gatherings.

Tending to Orientation Based Savagery and Separation:

An undeniable claim for ladies' booking is its capability to address orientation based viciousness and separation. Ladies in governmental issues frequently become advocates for legitimate changes and strategies that safeguard ladies' freedoms and security. The presence of ladies in regulative bodies can add to a more strong lawful structure that battles brutality against ladies, challenges biased practices, and encourages a cultural shift toward more prominent orien-tation balance.

Difficulties and Reactions:

Regardless of the unquestionable claims for ladies' booking, the proposition has confronted difficulties and reactions. Some contend that it might sustain posturing, with ladies involving seats without fundamentally affecting meaning-ful change. Pundits likewise express worries about the nature of administration, addressing whether held seats for ladies lead to viable approach execution and significant cultural change.

Catalyzing Social Movements:

One of the less substantial yet huge effects of ladies' booking is catalyzing social shifts potential. The perceivability of ladies in positions of authority challenges customary orientation jobs and generalizations.

As ladies demonstrate their abilities in administration, cultural mentalities to-ward ladies' jobs advance. This social change isn't restricted to metropolitan focuses yet penetrates provincial scenes, testing age-old insights and moving an age of little kids to try to influential places.

The Way Forward:

As India keeps on wrestling with the intricacies of a quickly influencing world, the case for ladies' booking stays significant and earnest. Endeavors should be coordinated toward upgrading the nature of portrayal, guaranteeing that ladies chiefs have the important assets, backing, and preparing to successfully explore the complexities of administration. Additionally, cultivating a climate that advances coordinated effort and inclusivity is pivotal for tackling the maximum capacity of different viewpoints inside authoritative bodies.

2. **Showcasing success stories and the impact of reservations**

As India wrestles with the basic of ladies' strengthening, the examples of overcoming adversity rising up out of the execution of reservations offer convincing accounts of change and progress. The effect of reservations, especially in political portrayal, has not just modified the segment scene of regulative bodies yet has additionally introduced unmistakable changes in approach detailing, grassroots turn of events, and cultural perspectives. By looking at these examples of overcoming adversity, one increases understanding into the capability of governmental policy regarding minorities in society to break down obstructions, challenge generalizations, and cultivate a more comprehensive and fair society.

Political Strengthening:

One of the main examples of overcoming adversity of ladies' reservations in India lies in the domain of political strengthening. The held seats for ladies at the neighborhood, state, and public levels have prompted a momentous expansion in the quantity of ladies in chosen positions. Ladies pioneers who have climbed to these jobs have broken the unattainable rank as well as become impetuses for change inside the political scene.

For example, the territory of Kerala has seen the positive effect of reservations through the rise of ladies pioneers like K. R. Gowri Amma, a pioneer who filled in as the Income Pastor and later as the Horticulture Priest. Such examples of overcoming adversity challenge customary thoughts about ladies' jobs in governmental issues and motivate people in the future to try to administrative roles.

Extraordinary Effect on Arrangements:

The effect of reservations goes past mathematical portrayal, stretching out to an extraordinary impact on strategies and administration. Ladies pioneers play played vital parts in forming regulation that resolves basic issues influencing ladies, kids, and underestimated networks. The held seats have become stages for promotion, giving voice to worries that were frequently underestimated or disregarded.

In the southern territory of Tamil Nadu, the booking strategy has added to the ascent of ladies pioneers like J. Jayalalithaa, who filled in as the Central Priest on numerous occasions. Her administration saw the execution of moderate approaches focused on ladies' strengthening, schooling, and social government assistance. These arrangement mediations mirror the significant effect that ladies' portrayal can have on tending to cultural difficulties and cultivating comprehensive turn of events.

Grassroots Initiative and Local area Improvement:

Held seats for ladies, especially at the Panchayat (neighborhood administration) level, have prompted a flood in grassroots authority. Ladies pioneers from different foundations play expected vital parts in dynamic cycles at the town and block levels. This grassroots strengthening has converted into local area driven improvement drives that address the particular requirements of the most weak fragments of society.

In states like Rajasthan, the booking strategy has enabled ladies pioneers to lead drives connected with wellbeing, schooling, and disinfection. Ladies drove Panchayats have been instrumental in carrying out projects that straightforwardly influence the prosperity of their networks. These examples of overcoming adversity highlight the significance of comprehensive administration and the capacity of ladies pioneers to drive positive change at the grassroots level.

Changing Cultural Mentalities:

One of the amazing effects of ladies' reservations is the slow yet huge change in cultural mentalities toward ladies in positions of authority. As ladies demonstrate their courage in administration, generalizations that once bound them to conventional jobs are progressively disintegrating. The examples of overcoming adversity of ladies pioneers have become strong stories testing instilled predispositions and rousing a social change.

In Uttar Pradesh, the appointment of Mayawati as the Central Pastor denoted a notable second, testing both orientation and standing based separation. Her example of overcoming adversity is a demonstration of the changing discernments about ladies' initiative capacities and their capacity to explore complex political scenes.

Instructive Strengthening and Job Demonstrating:

Ladies' reservations affect instructive strengthening. As ladies pioneers rise to places of impact, they become strong good examples, motivating little kids to seek after schooling and try to influential positions. The effect of reservations stretches out past legislative issues, impacting different circles of society, including the scholarly community.

For instance, the narrative of Anusuiya Uikey, who rose from a held seat in the Panchayat to turn into the Legislative head of Chhattisgarh, fills in as a motivation for endless little kids. Such examples of overcoming adversity challenge cultural standards and add to the destroying of orientation based hindrances in training and profession goals.

Financial Interest and Business venture:

Ladies' reservations play likewise had an impact in encouraging financial support and business venture. Ladies pioneers, outfitted with political impact, have upheld for arrangements and drives that help ladies in monetary undertakings. The examples of overcoming adversity in this area feature the diversity of reservations with more extensive objectives of financial strengthening.

In West Bengal, the initiative of Mamata Banerjee has seen an emphasis on ladies' monetary improvement through plans supporting business and expertise advancement. Such drives add to financial development as well as challenge orientation standards by extending ladies' jobs past conventional areas.

Challenges and Proceeded with Backing:

While examples of overcoming adversity flourish, the excursion toward orientation uniformity through reservations isn't without challenges. The persevering orientation based separation, cultural predispositions, and obstacles in exploring political scenes stay considerable deterrents. Proceeded with support for ladies' reservations is fundamental for address these difficulties and guarantee supported progress.

Chapter 1

The Status Quo of Women in India

The situation with ladies in India is a perplexing and multi-layered issue molded by verifiable, social, and financial elements. While the country has taken huge steps in different fields, steady moves and well established disparities keep on affecting the existences of ladies the nation over. Looking at business as usual of ladies in India requires an investigation of key spaces, including schooling, work, wellbeing, political portrayal, and the more extensive cultural perspectives that impact their encounters.

Instruction:

Training is many times thought about a foundation of strengthening, yet orientation variations endure in instructive fulfillment in India. While there has been prominent advancement in expanding in general education rates, orientation differentials remain especially articulated in specific districts and networks. Young ladies in provincial regions, having a place with minimized segments of society, frequently face obstructions like absence of access, cultural standards, and monetary requirements that limit their instructive open doors.

Endeavors to address these abberations have been in progress, with drives like the Sarva Shiksha Abhiyan expecting to further develop admittance to quality training for all. In any case, difficulties, for example, early marriage, orientation based savagery, and social standards that focus on young men's schooling keep on blocking the instructive progression of young ladies. Connecting the orientation hole in schooling is fundamental for breaking the pattern of destitution and empowering ladies to take part in the social and financial texture of the country effectively.

Business and Financial Interest:

The situation with ladies in the Indian labor force mirrors a division among progress and dug in orientation standards. While ladies have made advances into different callings and areas, they keep on confronting critical difficulties as far as compensation holes, word related isolation, and restricted open doors for professional success. The casual area, where a significant part of ladies is utilized, frequently needs employer stability, advantages, and roads for expertise improvement.

Additionally, the weight of neglected homegrown work and providing care liabilities lopsidedly falls on ladies, restricting their capacity to partake in conventional business completely. The common orientation standards and cultural assumptions add to a situation where ladies' monetary commitments are frequently underestimated. Tending to these difficulties requires extensive approaches that advance work environment fairness, address social predispositions, and perceive and rearrange the weight of homegrown obligations.

Wellbeing and Prosperity:

The wellbeing status of ladies in India is complicatedly connected to financial elements, social practices, and the accessibility of medical care administrations. Maternal death rates, however declining, stay higher than worldwide midpoints, showing determined difficulties in guaranteeing safe parenthood. Admittance to conceptive medical care, family arranging administrations, and mindfulness about regenerative freedoms keep on being regions that need consideration.

Orientation based savagery, including aggressive behavior at home, share related viciousness, and inappropriate behavior, presents huge dangers to the prosperity of ladies. The disgrace related with detailing such episodes, combined with deficient lawful components, frequently brings about underreporting and an absence of responsibility. Tending to the wellbeing and security of ladies requires a multi-pronged methodology that incorporates lawful changes, local area mindfulness, and the production of places of refuge for casualties.

Political Portrayal:

In spite of the booking strategies that expect to upgrade ladies' political support, the portrayal of ladies in administrative bodies stays nowhere near proportionate. While ladies have made progress in nearby administration through Panchayati Raj establishments, their presence in state governing bodies and public parliament is somewhat low.

Well established male centric standards, restricted admittance to assets, and the moves of exploring political scenes keep on blocking ladies' entrance into formal governmental issues.

While examples of overcoming adversity of ladies pioneers breaking obstructions exist, the more extensive story mirrors a requirement for supported endeavors to address the foundational boundaries that prevent ladies' political investment. Perceiving the significance of different voices in administration, proceeded with support for ladies' reservations and drives that advance ladies' political initiative are critical for making a more comprehensive political scene.

Cultural Mentalities and Social Standards:

The situation with ladies in India is unpredictably connected to cultural mentalities and social standards that shape orientation jobs and assumptions. Well established man centric qualities frequently propagate separation and build up conventional jobs for ladies. The inclination for male youngsters, reflected in sex-specific practices, keeps on winning in specific networks, prompting slanted sex proportions.

Besides, generalizations encompassing ladies' jobs and capacities add to a gendered division of work and restricted open doors for ladies in different circles. Changing cultural perspectives requires a purposeful work to challenge instilled inclinations, advance orientation sharpening, and enable ladies to overcome cultural presumption.

Legitimate Systems and Implementation:

India has gained ground in establishing regulation to safeguard and advance ladies' privileges, including regulations resolving issues like endowment, abusive behavior at home, and lewd behavior. Notwithstanding, the viability of these lawful structures frequently faces difficulties connected with execution, requirement, and cultural perspectives. The sluggish speed of equity, deficient emotionally supportive networks for casualties, and holes in legitimate assurances feature the requirement for nonstop endeavors to reinforce the lawful components that defend ladies' privileges.

1.1 Overview of gender disparities

Orientation differences address an inescapable and well established challenge that rises above geological limits, social settings, and financial variations. The term embodies the inconsistent treatment, open doors, and assumptions forced on people in view of their orientation. This outline of orientation abberations plans to dig into the diverse components of this issue, analyzing its verifiable roots, signs in various circles of life, and the continuous endeavors to address and correct these uneven characters.

Authentic Roots:

Orientation differences have verifiable predecessors profoundly implanted in friendly, social, and monetary designs. Customarily, social orders have been coordinated along man centric lines, where power, honor, and navigation were amassed in the possession of men. This authentic inheritance established the groundwork for orientation standards that recommended explicit jobs and assumptions for people, sustaining disparities across ages.

In many societies, ladies were appointed homegrown jobs, liable for providing care, while men were supposed to accept administrative roles in open arenas. These orientation standards restricted admittance to schooling, monetary open doors, and cooperation in community and political life for ladies. The verifiable foundations of orientation differences keep on applying effect on contemporary social orders, molding mentalities and sustaining unfair practices.

Financial Incongruities:

Orientation differences are distinctly apparent in monetary circles, where ladies face difficulties in getting to approach potential open doors, compensation, and professional success. The orientation pay hole, an unavoidable issue universally, mirrors the divergence in profit among people performing comparative jobs. This pay hole is in many cases a result of word related isolation, where certain callings are overwhelmed by one orientation, prompting undervaluation of work generally connected with ladies.

Also, ladies frequently endure the worst part of neglected homegrown work, restricting their capacity to take part completely in the proper labor force. The absence of admittance to monetary assets, credit, and enterprising open doors further adds to financial incongruities. Endeavors to connect these holes incorporate pushing for equivalent compensation, advancing working environment variety, and carrying out approaches that help balance between serious and fun activities.

Instructive Variations:

While critical headway has been made in advancing orientation correspondence in training, abberations continue in different locales and networks. In certain areas of the planet, young ladies actually face obstructions to getting to schooling, including social standards that focus on young men's schooling, early marriage, and restricted assets. Indeed, even in areas with generally high enlistment rates for young ladies, difficulties might emerge as far as nature of schooling, wellbeing concerns, and orientation predisposition in educational programs.

In tending to instructive variations, drives center around establishing comprehensive learning conditions, giving grants to young ladies, and testing generalizations that limit instructive yearnings. Schooling is viewed as an incredible asset for destroying orientation standards and enabling people to challenge and reshape cultural assumptions.

Wellbeing Differences:

Orientation differences in wellbeing envelop different aspects, including admittance to medical care administrations, maternal death rates, and regenerative freedoms. In certain areas, ladies face obstructions to getting to fundamental medical services, prompting variations in wellbeing results. Maternal death rates stay higher than satisfactory levels in specific regions, reflecting difficulties in guaranteeing safe parenthood and regenerative medical services.

Additionally, orientation based viciousness, including practices like female genital mutilation and youngster marriage, presents critical dangers to ladies' wellbeing. Endeavors to address wellbeing abberations center around further developing medical services openness, supporting for regenerative privileges, and battling orientation based viciousness through legitimate changes and mindfulness crusades.

Political Differences:

Political portrayal stays a space where orientation differences persevere internationally. Ladies are frequently underrepresented in administrative bodies, chief positions, and dynamic jobs. This underrepresentation restricts the variety of viewpoints and prevents the detailing of comprehensive strategies that address the requirements and worries of the whole populace.

Endeavors to address political variations incorporate governmental policy regarding minorities in society measures like quantities, held seats, and backing for ladies' co-operation in political authority. Expanding ladies' portrayal isn't just an issue of equity yet in addition an essential basic for cultivating more comprehensive and responsive administration.

Social and Social Differences:

Social and social standards assume a vital part in sustaining orientation variations. Generalizations and assumptions related with manliness and gentility shape people's jobs and breaking point their decisions. These standards can add to the standardization of orientation based savagery, separation, and inconsistent power elements in connections.

Social practices like settlement, honor killings, and limitations on ladies' versatility further build up orientation incongruities. Drives pointed toward testing these social standards incorporate instructive projects, mindfulness missions, and local area commitment to advance more evenhanded perspectives and ways of behaving.

Diversity of Inconsistencies:

It's pivotal to perceive that orientation inconsistencies converge with other social classes like race, nationality, class, and sexual direction, making complicated and layered types of separation. For instance, ladies of variety might confront intensified difficulties, encountering segregation in light of both their orientation and racial personality. Diversity underscores the requirement for extensive methodologies that address the interconnected idea of different types of disparity.

Worldwide Endeavors and Economical Improvement Objectives:

Addressing orientation differences is fundamental to the worldwide obligation to accomplishing the Reasonable Improvement Objectives (SDGs). Objective 5, explicitly, centers around accomplishing orientation balance and enabling all ladies and young ladies. Endeavors under this objective incorporate elevating equivalent admittance to schooling, finishing savagery and unsafe works on, guaranteeing equivalent support in direction, and tending to monetary abberations.

Worldwide associations, states, and common society drives work cooperatively to propel orientation uniformity. Promotion for strategy changes, legitimate changes, and grassroots developments add to the continuous endeavors to destroy orientation inconsistencies and construct an additional fair and impartial world.

1. **Educational inequalities**

   Instructive imbalances continue as a worldwide test, reflecting variations in access, quality, and results across different financial, geographic, and segment aspects. As social orders take a stab at progress and improvement, tending to these imbalances becomes basic for encouraging comprehensive development and guaranteeing that training fills in as an impetus for social portability as opposed to a perpetuator of social partitions. This investigation of instructive imbalances digs into the multi-layered nature of the issue, looking at its foundations, indications, and the continuous endeavors to connect these holes and make a more fair instructive scene.

   Foundations of Instructive Disparities:

   The foundations of instructive disparities are profoundly weaved with authentic, financial, and social variables. In numerous social orders, admittance to training has been molded by honor and power elements, bringing about fundamental boundaries for specific gatherings. Verifiable practices, like unfair arrangements, isolation, and restricted open doors, have left enduring engravings on school systems, making inconsistencies that continue across ages.

Monetary imbalances assume a critical part, as families with restricted monetary assets frequently face difficulties in giving quality schooling to their kids. This financial obstruction adds to a pattern of drawback, where people from monetarily underestimated foundations find it trying to break liberated from the limitations of restricted instructive open doors.

Social and social standards additionally add to instructive imbalances. Orientation predispositions, generalizations, and conventional assumptions about the jobs of various gatherings can prevent admittance to training and impact instructive decisions. Separation in light of race, identity, and position further mixtures the difficulties looked by minimized networks, restricting their admittance to instructive assets.

Admittance to Instruction:

One of the essential elements of instructive imbalances is inconsistent admittance to training. In many regions of the planet, especially in emerging nations, obstructions like absence of framework, deficient transportation, and geological distance limit admittance to schools. This is particularly obvious in country and minimized networks where instructive offices are scant, making it hard for kids to routinely go to class.

Orientation variations in access likewise endure, with young ladies confronting exceptional difficulties, for example, social standards that focus on young men's schooling, security concerns, and early marriage. Endeavors to address access issues incorporate structure foundation, giving transportation, and carrying out mindfulness missions to challenge social standards that ruin young ladies' schooling.

Nature of Training:

In any event, when access is free, abberations in the nature of training propagate disparities. Schools in monetarily hindered regions frequently miss the mark on assets, qualified educators, and refreshed educational programs. This outcomes in an instructive encounter that misses the mark concerning giving the essential abilities and information for understudies to flourish in a quickly impacting world.

Mechanical abberations further fuel the quality hole, with understudies in well-off regions or those with admittance to advanced assets enjoying an upper hand over their partners in less special networks. Crossing over the quality hole requires designated interests in educator preparing, foundation improvement, and the joining of innovation to guarantee that all understudies get a top notch schooling.

Financial Abberations:

Financial status keeps on being a huge determinant of instructive results. Kids from well-to-do families frequently approach non-public schools, customized mentoring, and extracurricular exercises, giving them an upper hand. Then again, understudies from monetarily hindered foundations might confront difficulties like deficient learning conditions, less instructive assets, and an absence of openness to different growth opportunities.

Advanced education, specifically, reflects financial inconsistencies, with understudies from advantaged foundations having more admittance to renowned establishments and better scholastic help. Tending to these variations includes carrying out governmental policy regarding minorities in society measures, giving monetary guide, and making pathways for understudies from minimized foundations to get to advanced education.

Worldwide Inconsistencies:

Instructive imbalances are not bound to explicit districts but rather manifest all around the world. Inconsistencies among created and agricultural nations feature the difficulties looked by countries with restricted assets. The worldwide computerized partition worsens these holes, with understudies in prosperous nations profiting from cutting edge mechanical assets, while understudies in less evolved districts battle to get to essential instructive apparatuses.

Endeavors to address worldwide instructive disparities include global joint efforts, help projects, and drives that focus on training as a central common liberty. Connecting worldwide differences requires a promise to feasible improvement objectives and guaranteeing that schooling is focused on in global plans.

Effect of Instructive Disparities:

The effect of instructive disparities stretches out a long ways past the limits of the study hall. Restricted admittance to quality instruction hampers social portability, propagates patterns of destitution, and builds up existing social orders. People who face instructive weaknesses frequently experience hindrances in getting to monetary open doors, partaking in municipal life, and appreciating in general prosperity.

Besides, instructive imbalances add to an information hole that broadens financial variations. In a quickly developing worldwide economy, people with deficient training find themselves unfit to explore the intricacies of the cutting edge labor force, frustrating their true capacity for individual and expert development.

Endeavors to Address Instructive Imbalances:

Perceiving the earnestness of tending to instructive disparities, legislatures, non-administrative associations, and instructive foundations are executing a scope of mediations to connect these holes. Designated strategies, governmental policy regarding minorities in society measures, and local area commitment drives mean to make a more comprehensive instructive scene.

Grant programs and monetary guide mean to make training more available for understudies from financially burdened foundations. Interests in framework, educator preparing, and educational plan advancement add to working on the nature of training in underserved regions. Governmental policy regarding minorities in society arrangements, for example, held seats for minimized networks, try to review authentic treacheries and advance variety in instructive establishments.

2. **Workplace discrimination**

Working environment separation stays an unavoidable issue that rises above ventures, topographical limits, and social settings.

In spite of progressions in mindfulness and legitimate systems, oppressive practices continue, frustrating the accomplishment of comprehensive and impartial workplaces. This investigation dives into the mind boggling elements of work environment segregation, looking at its different structures, fundamental causes, and the continuous endeavors to kill such inclinations from the expert domain.

Types of Working environment Separation:

Working environment separation can appear in different structures, setting out hindrances to approach open doors and propagating disparity. The most widely recognized types include:

Orientation Separation: Orientation based segregation is predominant in working environments around the world. It includes inconsistent compensation, one-sided employing practices, and generalizations that breaking point professional success for people in view of their orientation. The discriminatory limitation peculiarity, where ladies experience boundaries in arriving at administrative roles, shows the steadiness of orientation segregation.

Racial and Ethnic Separation: Segregation in light of race and identity stays a huge test in numerous working environments. People from minimized racial or ethnic gatherings might confront predispositions in employing, advancement, and everyday associations. Negligible hostilities, racial profiling, and exclusionary rehearses add to an unpleasant workplace.

Age Separation: Ageism can influence both more youthful and more established workers. More youthful people might experience generalizations connected with naiveté, while more seasoned laborers might confront difficulties, for example, being disregarded for advancements or encountering inconspicuous predispositions that subvert their commitments.

Incapacity Segregation: People with handicaps frequently defy biased rehearses connected with recruiting, availability, and sensible convenience. Pessimistic discernments about the capacities of individuals with incapacities can prompt rejection and restricted professional success open doors.

Sexual Direction and Orientation Personality Separation: Segregation in view of sexual direction or orientation character can make a threatening working environment for individuals from the LGBTQ+ people group. Biases, provocation, and absence of comprehensive strategies add to a workplace where people might feel a sense of urgency to hide their character.

Basic Reasons for Work environment Separation:
Understanding the hidden reasons for working environment separation is fundamental for concocting viable procedures to resolve these issues. A few elements add to the propagation of prejudicial practices:

Certain Predisposition: Understood inclination alludes to oblivious mentalities or generalizations that impact direction. In recruiting, advancement, and everyday communications, people may unconsciously hold onto predispositions in light of race, orientation, or different qualities, affecting their decisions and ways of behaving.

Hierarchical Culture: The way of life inside an association assumes a vital part in forming perspectives toward variety and consideration. A culture that encourages inclusivity, regard, and rise to valuable open doors can relieve segregation, while a harmful or unfair culture sustains inclinations.

Absence of Variety Drives: Associations that don't focus on variety and consideration may accidentally sustain prejudicial practices. Nonappearance of designated drives, mentorship projects, and racial awareness coaching can add to a climate where inclinations go ignored.

Lacking Strategies and Implementation: Powerless or ineffectively upheld hostile to segregation arrangements add to a lenient climate for unfair ways of behaving. At the point when people see an absence of ramifications for unfair activities, it encourages such practices.

Generalizations and Biases: Firmly established generalizations and biases about specific gatherings add to prejudicial ways of behaving. Generalizing propagates thin and one-sided points of view that thwart people from different foundations in their expert development.

Effect of Work environment Separation:
Work environment separation has expansive results that stretch out past the person to influence authoritative elements and by and large efficiency. A portion of the key effects include:

Diminished Spirit and Efficiency: People who experience segregation frequently face close to home trouble, prompting diminished resolve and occupation fulfillment. This, thusly, influences efficiency and by and large work environment air.

High Turnover Rates: Segregation can drive skilled representatives to look for business somewhere else, adding to high turnover rates. The deficiency of talented people lessens hierarchical viability and upsets group elements.

Restricted Variety and Advancement: Unfair practices impede the consideration of different viewpoints, restricting imagination and development inside the work environment. Different groups are known to be more imaginative, versatile, and fit for critical thinking.

Lawful Outcomes: Segregation in the work environment can bring about legitimate ramifications for associations. Claims, fines, and harm to notoriety are potential results when biased rehearses are uncovered and tended to through legitimate channels.

Negative Authoritative Standing: Working environment segregation discolors an association's standing both inside and remotely. Negative audits, online entertainment kickback, and the dispersal of biased practices can hurt the association's remaining in the business and among likely representatives.

Endeavors to Battle Working environment Segregation:

Combatting work environment separation requires a complex methodology that includes people, associations, and regulative bodies. Key endeavors include:

Variety and Incorporation Projects: Associations can execute variety and consideration programs that go past way of talking to encourage a comprehensive culture effectively. These projects might incorporate instructional courses, mentorship drives, and arrangements that focus on variety at all levels.

Hostile to Segregation Strategies: Clear and thorough enemy of separation strategies are fundamental for laying out a system that disallows prejudicial practices. These approaches ought to be discussed actually, with systems set up for announcing and tending to separation.

Preparing and Schooling: Associations can direct ordinary instructional meetings to bring issues to light about oblivious inclinations, generalizations, and the effect of oppressive practices. Preparing projects ought to underline the significance of variety and consideration in establishing a positive work environment climate.

Legitimate Securities: Official bodies assume a significant part in giving lawful assurances against work environment separation. Strong enemy of separation regulations, alongside compelling requirement components, engage people to look for plan of action while confronting unfair practices.

Advancing Comprehensive Initiative: Administration that effectively advances inclusivity establishes the vibe for the whole association. Comprehensive pioneers focus on variety, model comprehensive ways of behaving, and encourage a climate where each individual feels esteemed and heard.

3. **Cultural and societal barriers**

Social and cultural boundaries comprise a diverse web that frequently sustains imbalance and hinders progress toward an additional comprehensive and fair world. Established in authentic standards, social customs, and cultural assumptions, these boundaries shape people's encounters and potential open doors, making differences across different aspects. This investigation dives into the multifaceted elements of social and cultural boundaries, analyzing their signs, fundamental causes, and the continuous endeavors to destroy these obstacles to advance.

Signs of Social and Cultural Hindrances:

Orientation Jobs and Assumptions:

Social standards frequently direct inflexible orientation jobs and assumptions, affecting people's way of behaving, decisions, and open doors. Ladies, in numerous social orders, face limitations that limit their admittance to training, vocation decisions, and positions of authority. Alternately, men might experience cultural strain to adjust to conventional ideas of manliness, limiting their appearance of feelings or quest for contemporary vocations.

Rank and Class Pecking orders:

In many societies, particularly in South Asia, rank frameworks have generally molded social designs, making ordered progressions that decide people's admittance to assets, training, and business open doors. Additionally, class qualifications propagate monetary disparities, restricting social portability and building up honor for those in higher social layers.

Racial and Ethnic Segregation:

Racial and ethnic biases implanted in social accounts add to segregation, predisposition, and fundamental disparities. People from minimized racial or ethnic gatherings might confront hindrances in training, business, and social communications because of firmly established generalizations and predispositions that continue inside social orders.

LGBTQ+ Disgrace:

Cultural standards frequently deride people who distinguish as LGBTQ+, making obstructions to acknowledgment, equivalent privileges, and admittance to different open doors. Segregation and prohibition in light of sexual direction or orientation character can bring about emotional wellness challenges, restricted work prospects, and limited social mix.

Ageism:

Social perspectives toward age can prompt age-based segregation, affecting people at different life stages. More established people might confront inclinations that limit their vocation possibilities, while more youthful people might experience suspicion about their abilities and experience. Ageism impacts employing choices, professional success, and impression of ability.

Fundamental Reasons for Social and Cultural Hindrances:

Well established Customs:

Social obstructions frequently originate from well established customs and cultural standards that have persevered over ages. Testing these instilled convictions requires a nuanced approach that regards social legacy while advancing a more comprehensive translation of custom.

Absence of Schooling and Mindfulness:

Obliviousness and absence of mindfulness add to the propagation of social and cultural boundaries. In people group where admittance to schooling is restricted, falsehood and generalizations persevere, ruining progress toward additional liberal and comprehensive social orders.

Anxiety toward Change:

Cultural protection from change can be a huge hindrance. Apprehension about upsetting laid out standards and customs might prompt obstruction against endeavors to challenge prejudicial practices. Upholding for change requires exploring this obstruction and cultivating discourse to address concerns and misguided judgments.

Monetary Variations:

Monetary variations are firmly entwined with social and cultural obstructions. Restricted admittance to assets, schooling, and valuable open doors sustains patterns of destitution and supports existing social orders. Tending to monetary disparities is fundamental for destroying more extensive social and cultural obstructions.

Absence of Portrayal:

The shortfall of different voices in dynamic cycles adds to the propagation of social and cultural boundaries. At the point when underestimated bunches need portrayal in places of impact, their viewpoints and necessities might go ignored, further settling in disparities.

Endeavors to Destroy Social and Cultural Boundaries:

Social Responsiveness and Instruction:

Advancing social responsiveness through training and mindfulness crusades is vital for destroying obstructions. Instructive drives that challenge generalizations, feature assorted points of view, and encourage a comprehension of various societies add to making more comprehensive social orders.

Legitimate Changes and Assurances:

Establishing and implementing legitimate securities against segregation is key to destroying cultural hindrances. Powerful enemy of separation regulations and strategies give a structure to testing prejudicial practices and considering people and foundations responsible for their activities.

Portrayal and Inclusivity:

Expanding portrayal of minimized bunches in different areas is a strong methodology for separating social and cultural boundaries. At the point when people from different foundations are available in dynamic jobs, their encounters and viewpoints can impact strategies and practices.

Local area Commitment and Exchange:

Drawing in networks in open discourse encourages understanding and difficulties imbued predispositions. Local area based drives that empower discussions about social standards, generalizations, and unfair practices add to destroying boundaries from the grassroots level.

Advancing Variety in Media:

Media assumes a critical part in forming social stories. Advancing variety in media portrayal helps challenge generalizations and gives a stage to stories that mirror the extravagance and intricacy of different societies and personalities.

Difficulties and Future Points of view:

Protection from Change:

Beating protection from change stays a huge test. People and networks acclimated with specific social standards might oppose endeavors to challenge prejudicial works on, seeing them as dangers to their lifestyle. Building scaffolds of understanding and underlining the common advantages of inclusivity are fundamental methodologies.

Diversity:

Perceiving the diversity of social and cultural hindrances is vital. People frequently face different types of separation in light of their orientation, race, class, or different characters. Tending to these converging boundaries requires far reaching approaches that think about the intricacy of people's encounters.

Worldwide Coordinated effort:

Social and cultural obstructions are not bound to explicit districts but rather are worldwide peculiarities. Cooperative endeavors on a global scale, including legislatures, associations, and grassroots developments, are fundamental for tending to foundational imbalances and destroying hindrances on a more extensive scale.

Proceeded with Instruction:

Consistent schooling and mindfulness building endeavors are essential for supporting advancement. Social and cultural mentalities develop after some time, and progressing instruction is crucial for testing generalizations, advancing inclusivity, and adjusting to the changing necessities of assorted social orders.

1.2 Statistics and illustrating the challenges

In understanding the complicated scene of imbalance, measurements act as incredible assets, offering bits of knowledge into the unavoidable difficulties looked by different networks all over the planet.

From monetary abberations to instructive access, looking at the information permits us to get a handle on the profundity and broadness of cultural lopsided characteristics. This investigation dives into key insights that outline the difficulties of imbalance, traversing different aspects like pay, instruction, medical services, and portrayal, revealing insight into the tenacious holes that keep on forming the encounters of people and networks.

Pay Disparity:

One of the most over the top glaring appearances of imbalance is pay uniqueness, where the dissemination of abundance inside social orders reflects fundamental lopsided characteristics. As per a report by the World Imbalance Lab, starting around 2022, the top 1% of the worldwide populace holds two times as much abundance as the base half. This stunning measurement highlights the convergence of monetary assets in the possession of a chosen handful, propagating patterns of destitution and restricting open doors for social versatility.

Inside countries, pay imbalance shows unmistakably. In the US, for instance, the top 1% of pay workers represented over 20% of absolute pre-charge pay lately, as per information from the World Riches and Pay Data set. Such variations add to social turmoil, block the accomplishment of equivalent open doors, and highlight the dire requirement for strategies that address abundance rearrangement and advance monetary inclusivity.

Instructive Inconsistencies:

Schooling fills in as a foundation for social portability and equivalent admittance to valuable open doors. Notwithstanding, worldwide measurements uncover relentless instructive variations that obstruct the acknowledgment of these beliefs. As per UNESCO, around 258 million kids and young people overall were out of school in 2020. This measurement features the difficulties of guaranteeing general admittance to training, especially in locales wrestling with monetary unsteadiness, struggle, and orientation based segregation.

Orientation based instructive inconsistencies stay a huge test. As per the Worldwide Organization for Schooling, in some low-pay nations, young ladies are more averse to finish essential training contrasted with young men. The orientation hole further enlarges at advanced education levels, restricting ladies' admittance to ability improvement and financial open doors.

Medical services Inconsistencies:

Admittance to medical services is an essential right, yet obvious incongruities endure worldwide. As per the World Wellbeing Association (WHO), starting around 2022, a large number of individuals need admittance to fundamental wellbeing administrations. In low-pay nations, the difficulties are exacerbated, with restricted assets and framework obstructing the arrangement of satisfactory medical care.

Maternal death rates act as an impactful sign of medical services differences. As per UNICEF, maternal death rates in sub-Saharan Africa are roughly 534 passings for every 100,000 live births, contrasted with 11 passings for each 100,000 live births in big league salary nations. These measurements highlight the basic requirement for designated intercessions to address medical care imbalances and guarantee that all people, no matter what their financial status, approach quality wellbeing administrations.

Racial and Ethnic Abberations:

Racial and ethnic inconsistencies persevere across different areas, reflecting foundational predispositions and oppressive practices. In the US, for example, measurements uncover glaring holes in regions like law enforcement, work, and medical services. As per the American Common Freedoms Association (ACLU), Dark people are multiple times as liable to be captured for drug ownership contrasted with their white partners, notwithstanding comparable use rates.

In the working environment, racial differences are obvious in wage holes and portrayal in administrative roles. As per information from the U.S. Agency of Work Insights, starting around 2022, the middle week by week income for Dark and Hispanic specialists are lower than those for white laborers. Besides, a report by the Middle for Ability Development features the "broken rung" peculiarity, demonstrating that racial and ethnic minorities face hindrances to progression, with restricted portrayal in the initial step to administrative jobs.

Orientation Incongruities:

Orientation imbalance perseveres around the world, influencing different parts of life, from financial investment to political portrayal. As per the World Monetary Discussion's Worldwide Orientation Hole Report 2021, the orientation hole in financial support and opportunity stays wide, with just 58% of this hole shut universally. As far as political strengthening, ladies are fundamentally underrepresented, holding just 26.1% of parliamentary seats around the world.

Working environment oppression ladies is a persevering test. By and large, 16% not as much as men around the world, as indicated by the Global Work Association (ILO). Prejudicial practices, restricted open doors for professional success, and the inconsistent weight of providing care liabilities add to these abberations, highlighting the requirement for far reaching endeavors to accomplish orientation fairness.

Portrayal Incongruities:

Portrayal in dynamic jobs stays a significant part of tending to more extensive cultural disparities. Notwithstanding progress, different gatherings keep on being underrepresented in, influential places and impact. As indicated by the Between Parliamentary Association, starting around 2021, ladies address just 26.7% of the world's parliamentarians. This absence of portrayal blocks the definition of comprehensive arrangements and builds up orientation standards that propagate imbalance.

Essentially, racial and ethnic minorities frequently experience underrepresentation in political and corporate administration. In the US, information from the Middle for American Ladies and that's what governmental issues shows, starting around 2022, just 23.7% of U.S. legislative seats are held by minorities. These measurements highlight the requirement for purposeful endeavors to separate boundaries and make pathways for people from different foundations to accept influential positions.

Challenges in Tending to Disparity:

Tending to imbalance is an intricate errand that requires multi-layered methodologies and a pledge to fundamental change. A few difficulties hinder progress in this undertaking:

Protection from Change:

Cultural protection from change represents a critical test. Settled in social standards, financial interests, and the apprehension about losing honors add to opposition against arrangements pointed toward destroying fundamental imbalances. Beating this obstruction requires tenacious promotion, training, and local area commitment.

Absence of Exhaustive Approaches:

At times, piecemeal approaches address explicit parts of disparity without handling the underlying drivers. An absence of complete and diverse strategies ruins the formation of a comprehensive system that tends to the interconnected idea of different types of segregation.

Lacking Portrayal:

The absence of portrayal of underestimated bunches in dynamic cycles stays a test. Without assorted voices at the table, strategies may not satisfactorily mirror the requirements and encounters of various networks, propagating abberations.

Worldwide Collaboration:

In a universally interconnected world, tending to disparity requires global participation. Be that as it may, international difficulties, contrasting needs, and monetary interests frequently obstruct cooperative endeavors to make a more impartial worldwide request.

Restricted Admittance to Assets:

Restricted admittance to assets, especially in low-pay networks, worsens existing disparities. Lacking interest in training, medical services, and financial open doors sustains patterns of weakness and hinders progress toward balance.

Chapter 2

Affirmative Action: A Historical Perspective

Governmental policy regarding minorities in society, as a strategy approach, has been an essential instrument in tending to verifiable and fundamental disparities by giving designated chances to minimized gatherings. Starting in the US during the twentieth hundred years, governmental policy regarding minorities in society planned to redress the profoundly imbued differences that generally hindered racial and ethnic minorities, ladies, and other underrepresented gatherings. This verifiable point of view investigates the advancement of governmental policy regarding minorities in society, following its foundations, analyzing critical minutes, and evaluating its effect on cultural elements.

Starting points of Governmental policy regarding minorities in society:

The starting points of governmental policy regarding minorities in society can be followed back to the social equality development in the US during the 1960s. The development looked to destroy organized prejudice and separation that plagued different parts of American culture, especially in schooling and work.

As a reaction to settled in imbalances, President John F. Kennedy presented the expression "governmental policy regarding minorities in society" in Chief Request 10925 of every 1961, which planned to guarantee that governmentally subsidized undertakings would find certifiable ways to advance equivalent open door and dispense with unfair practices.

In any case, it was President Lyndon B. Johnson who hardened and extended the idea with the issuance of Chief Request 11246 of every 1965. This request commanded that government project workers make a confirmed move to guarantee that candidates are utilized and that representatives are treated during work regardless of their race, variety, religion, sex, or public beginning. This noticeable a critical stage toward tending to verifiable disparities by effectively advancing variety and incorporation.

Governmental policy regarding minorities in society in Advanced education:

Governmental policy regarding minorities in society found perhaps of its most conspicuous application in the domain of advanced education. Milestone High Legal disputes formed the direction of governmental policy regarding minorities in society arrangements, with the essential instance of Officials of the College of California v. Bakke in 1978 being especially persuasive. For this situation, the Court decided that while unbending racial quantities were illegal, race could be thought of as one of a few elements in college confirmations cycles to accomplish a different understudy body.

Resulting cases, like Grutter v. Bollinger (2003) and Fisher v. College of Texas at Austin (2016), further explained the boundaries of governmental policy regarding minorities in society in school affirmations. These choices highlighted the significance of variety as a convincing state interest, gave that race-cognizant strategies are barely custom-made and utilized as one component among numerous in a comprehensive confirmations process.

Governmental policy regarding minorities in society in Work:

Governmental policy regarding minorities in society in business has been instrumental in breaking down boundaries and advancing equivalent open doors in the labor force. The Workplace of Government Agreement Consistence Projects (OFCCP) supervises governmental policy regarding minorities in society arrangements for bureaucratic project workers, guaranteeing consistence with against segregation measures. Managers under these guidelines are expected to find proactive ways to address underrepresentation and advance variety.

The objectives of governmental policy regarding minorities in society in business incorporate expanding the portrayal of ladies, racial and ethnic minorities, people with handicaps, and veterans in the labor force. Organizations are frequently expected to set explicit employing targets and effectively carry out effort and enrollment drives to draw in different ability. While pundits contend that governmental policy regarding minorities in society can be opposite separation, defenders keep up with that it is an important device to redress verifiable treacheries and make comprehensive work environments.

Difficulties and Reactions:

Governmental policy regarding minorities in society has confronted steady difficulties and reactions over now is the right time. One essential analysis revolves around the thought of opposite segregation, declaring that governmental policy regarding minorities in society approaches can hindrance people who don't have a place with generally underestimated gatherings. Pundits contend that merit-based standards ought to be the sole determinants in affirmations or employing processes.

Another test is the changing lawful scene, with some court choices restricting the extent of governmental policy regarding minorities in society approaches. The instance of Fisher v. College of Texas at Austin, for instance, put a higher weight on instructive organizations to exhibit that race-cognizant confirmations strategies are important to accomplish variety. Such lawful difficulties have prompted continuous discussions about the legality and viability of governmental policy regarding minorities in society.

Also, governmental policy regarding minorities in society has been censured for not tending to the main drivers of disparity, for example, deficient essential and optional schooling in underserved networks. Pundits contend that zeroing in on governmental policy regarding minorities in society without resolving foundational issues propagates a pattern of weakness.

Influence on Variety and Incorporation:

While governmental policy regarding minorities in society has confronted difficulties, its effect on variety and consideration can't be put into words. In schooling, governmental policy regarding minorities in society has added to more assorted understudy bodies, cultivating a rich gaining climate where understudies from various foundations can participate in significant communications and expand their viewpoints. Studies have shown that openness to variety in instructive settings prompts positive results, including worked on decisive reasoning and critical thinking abilities.

In the labor force, governmental policy regarding minorities in society plays made light of a part in breaking hindrances and advancing variety at different degrees of associations. Organizations with vigorous governmental policy regarding minorities in society strategies will generally have more comprehensive working environment societies, profiting from a large number of points of view and encounters. This variety isn't just a question of civil rights yet is progressively perceived as an upper hand in a globalized and interconnected world.

Development in the 21st 100 years:

In the 21st hundred years, governmental policy regarding minorities in society keeps on developing because of changing cultural elements. The center has extended to address race and nationality as well as orientation, sexual direction, incapacity status, and different components of variety. The more extensive origination of variety mirrors a comprehension that numerous variables add to the intricacy of people's encounters and characters.

As of late, the discussion around governmental policy regarding minorities in society has stretched out past conventional racial classes to envelop issues like financial status and geological portrayal. This more extensive methodology recognizes that people from financially impeded foundations might confront obstructions to access and opportunity, regardless of whether they fit flawlessly into customary classes of underrepresentation.

In addition, the multifacetedness of characters has acquired unmistakable quality in conversations about governmental policy regarding minorities in society. Perceiving that people might encounter numerous types of segregation in light of the crossing point of their race, orientation, and different personalities has prompted a more nuanced and comprehensive comprehension of variety.

Worldwide Points of view on Governmental policy regarding minorities in society:

Governmental policy regarding minorities in society arrangements and their counterparts are not novel to the US; they exist in different structures worldwide. Nations like India, South Africa, and Brazil have carried out governmental policy regarding minorities in society measures to address verifiable imbalances and advance inclusivity.

In India, for instance, the booking framework designates a specific level of government occupations and instructive open doors to explicit standings and clans that have generally confronted separation. Essentially, South Africa executed governmental policy regarding minorities in society strategies present politically-sanctioned racial segregation on change authentic uneven characters and advance portrayal for the recently minimized Dark populace.

2.1 Evolution of reservation policies in India

India, a country set apart by its rich social variety, has wrestled with verifiable disparities profoundly implanted in its social texture. Because of hundreds of years of segregation and mistreatment, the Indian government has executed reservation strategies as an essential device to elevate minimized networks and address verifiable treacheries. This investigation follows the advancement of reservation arrangements in India, analyzing their verifiable roots, key achievements, and the continuous discussions encompassing their execution.

Authentic Roots:

The underlying foundations of reservation strategies in India can be followed back to the arrangement of position based separation, a profoundly settled in friendly order that consigned specific gatherings to the edges of society. By and large, people having a place with Booked Standings (SCs), Planned Clans (STs), and Other In reverse Classes (OBCs) confronted fundamental prohibition, monetary hardship, and social minimization.

The composers of the Indian Constitution perceived the criticalness of amending these authentic treacheries. Dr. B.R. Ambedkar, a critical designer of the Constitution and a hero of civil rights, assumed an essential part in consolidating arrangements to elevate the minimized.

The Constitution of India, embraced in 1950, established the groundwork for governmental policy regarding minorities in society with arrangements for reservation of seats in instructive organizations and government occupations for SCs and STs under Articles 15(4) and 16(4).

Key Achievements:

First Alteration (1951):

The Primary Revision to the Indian Constitution in 1951 denoted a significant achievement in the development of reservation strategies. It explained the state's position to make exceptional arrangements for the progression of socially and instructively in reverse classes, empowering the public authority to start governmental policy regarding minorities in society measures.

Mandal Commission (1980):

The Mandal Commission, authoritatively known as the Second In reverse Classes Commission, was comprised in 1979 to recognize the socially and instructively in reverse classes and suggest measures for their progression. The Commission, led by

B.P. Mandal, presented its report in 1980, suggesting a 27% booking for OBCs in instructive establishments and government occupations. The Mandal Commission's suggestions blended critical discussion and fights, yet the public authority, drove by State head V.P. Singh, carried out the Mandal Commission's report in 1990.

Indra Sawhney Case (1992):

The execution of the Mandal Commission suggestions confronted lawful difficulties, prompting the milestone judgment in the Indra Sawhney case in 1992. The High Court maintained the idea of reservations however forced a cap of half, keeping portions from surpassing portion of the accessible seats. The court additionally decided that financial rules couldn't be the sole reason for reservations.

77th and 103rd Sacred Alterations:

The 77th Amendment (1995) permitted states to give reservations in advancements to SCs and STs in government occupations. Hence, the 103rd Amendment (2019) presented another arrangement, Article 15(6), permitting the public authority to give reservations to monetarily more vulnerable segments (EWS) as well as existing bookings for SCs, STs, and OBCs.

Discussions and Reactions:

In spite of the respectable expectation of reservation strategies, they have been a subject of progressing discussion and analysis. One significant disputed matter spins around the idea of "velvety layer," wherein people from held classifications who have achieved a specific degree of financial or instructive status are prohibited from the advantages of reservations. Pundits contend that barring the rich layer is fundamental to guarantee that the advantages arrive at the individuals who need them the most.

One more analysis focuses on the propagation of station based personalities. Pundits fight that reservations in view of position propagate and try and support the standing framework as opposed to destroying it. The contention places that a shift towards monetary standards as opposed to rank contemplations could be a more compelling method for tending to social and financial variations.

Also, there are worries about the effect of reservations on meritocracy. Adversaries contend that the accentuation on station based reservations might think twice about nature of instruction and labor force, as applicants might be chosen in light of their rank as opposed to their capacities and capabilities.

Extension of Reservations:

Throughout the long term, the extent of reservations in India has extended to address arising difficulties and evolving financial elements. The presentation of bookings for EWS in 2019 denoted a huge takeoff from the conventional spotlight on standing based reservations. This extension mirrors an affirmation that financial disserve, paying little heed to rank, is a hindrance to open doors and should be tended to.

The booking strategies have additionally stretched out to different areas past schooling and government occupations. Reservations are currently carried out in nearby bodies, regulative congregations, and Parliament to guarantee political portrayal for underestimated networks. Furthermore, public area undertakings and confidential organizations have been urged to intentionally take on reservation approaches.

Influence on Schooling:

Reservation strategies significantly affect instructive open doors for generally minimized networks. They have worked with expanded admittance to schooling for SCs, STs, and OBCs, making a more comprehensive advanced education scene. Subsequently, people from these networks have had the option to break the pattern of destitution and add to the financial improvement of their networks.

In any case, challenges continue guaranteeing that the advantages of reservations convert into worked on instructive results. Issues like deficient essential and auxiliary training, absence of foundation, and financial differences keep on thwarting the full acknowledgment of the capability of reservation arrangements in the schooling area.

Financial and Work Suggestions:

Reservation strategies in government occupations play had a significant impact in expanding portrayal from minimized networks in open area business. The strategies have helped in tending to verifiable uneven characters and making a more different and comprehensive labor force. Notwithstanding, challenges remain, including worries about the underrepresentation of specific gatherings inside held classes and the requirement for successful execution to guarantee that the planned advantages arrive at the meriting competitors.

In the confidential area, the reception of reservation approaches has been less uniform. While certain organizations have deliberately embraced variety and incorporation drives, others have been reluctant to execute quantities, refering to worries about meritocracy and functional effectiveness. Advocates contend that expanded variety in the corporate area isn't just an issue of civil rights yet in addition an upper hand that encourages development and imagination.

The Street Ahead:

As India explores the intricacies of reservation strategies, there is a developing acknowledgment that an extensive methodology is required. Past reservations, tending to the main drivers of disparity, like further developing admittance to quality schooling, medical services, and financial open doors, is fundamental. Policymakers, researchers, and activists keep on investigating inventive answers for make a more fair society.

Endeavors to find some kind of harmony between position based reservations and financial models are in progress, with conversations about the requirement for a more nuanced approach. The attention on monetary rules means to stretch out advantages to monetarily burdened people across ranks while recognizing that station based separation perseveres.

The fate of reservation arrangements in India likewise depends on the capacity to adjust to changing socioeconomics and arising difficulties. A dynamic and comprehensive methodology that thinks about interconnection, embraces variety, and addresses the developing necessities of minimized networks is critical for the proceeded with pertinence and viability of these strategies.

1. **Caste-based reservations**

   Position based reservations stand as a particular element of India's governmental policy regarding minorities in society strategies, pointed toward tending to extremely old social orders and encouraging inclusivity. Established in verifiable separation, the booking framework looks to elevate underestimated networks by furnishing them with admittance to instructive open doors, government occupations, and political portrayal. This investigation digs into the diverse components of standing based reservations in India, following their authentic beginnings, evaluating their effect on society, and looking at the continuous difficulties and discussions that encompass this complicated strategy system.

Verifiable Beginnings:

The foundations of position based reservations can be followed back to the inescapable station framework that has ruled Indian culture for a really long time. The position situation, described by inflexible social progressive systems and innate occupations, prompted the minimization and abuse of specific gatherings, quite the Planned Ranks (SCs), Booked Clans (STs), and socially and instructively in reverse classes.

The designers of the Indian Constitution perceived the requirement for governmental policy regarding minorities in society to amend authentic shameful acts. Dr. B.R. Ambedkar, himself a promoter for the freedoms of the minimized and a vital engineer of the Constitution, assumed a crucial part in consolidating arrangements for reservation in instructive establishments and government occupations under Articles 15(4) and 16(4). The objective was to break the shackles of exceptionally old separation and give open doors to social and financial upliftment.

Execution and Development:

The execution of rank based reservations picked up speed in the post-autonomy period, with progressive states sanctioning approaches to elevate SCs, STs, and Other In reverse Classes (OBCs). The Mandal Commission, shaped in 1979 to distinguish socially and instructively in reverse classes, suggested a 27% booking for OBCs in instructive establishments and government occupations. Notwithstanding confronting opposition and fights, the public authority, under State leader V.P. Singh, carried out the Mandal Commission's proposals in 1990.

The Indra Sawhney case in 1992 denoted a huge legitimate achievement, where the High Court maintained the idea of reservations however forced a cap of half. The court stressed that reservations shouldn't surpass half of the accessible seats and decided that monetary measures alone couldn't be the reason for reservations. These legitimate improvements formed the direction of standing based reservations, illustrating the shapes inside which governmental policy regarding minorities in society strategies would work.

Influence on Training:

Standing based reservations groundbreakingly affect instructive open doors for minimized networks. By saving seats in instructive foundations, the strategies expected to break the pattern of intergenerational impediment and give a pathway to people from SC, ST, and OBC foundations to get to advanced education.

While the effect has been critical, challenges endure. The nature of essential and auxiliary schooling in many underestimated networks remains below average, influencing the readiness of understudies to seek held seats in advanced education. Also, there are worries about the centralization of reservations in unambiguous disciplines, prompting underrepresentation in fields like science and innovation.

Notwithstanding these difficulties, the booking framework has added to expanded enlistment of understudies from generally minimized foundations in advanced education. It has likewise prompted the development of another age of experts, separating boundaries and testing customary stories of avoidance.

Work Amazing open doors and Financial Upliftment:

Position based reservations in government occupations have been instrumental in tending to authentic irregular characteristics in business open doors.

By holding an extent of government positions for SCs, STs, and OBCs, the strategies plan to guarantee that public area work mirrors the variety of the populace.

The booking arrangements have worked with financial upliftment by giving stable business potential open doors to people from underestimated networks. Admittance to government occupations, which frequently accompany advantages and professional stability, affects the financial states of families, adding to the more extensive objective of breaking the pattern of destitution.

In any case, concerns have been raised about the underrepresentation of specific gatherings inside the saved classes and the requirement for additional far reaching measures to address financial differences. The idea of the "rich layer" has been acquainted with bar financially well-off people inside saved classifications from the advantages of reservations, guaranteeing that the advantages arrive at the individuals who need them the most.

Difficulties and Reactions:

While station based reservations have been a basic instrument for civil rights, they have likewise been dependent upon analysis and discussion. One essential analysis spins around the propagation of rank characters. Pundits contend that by zeroing in on rank based reservations, the strategies coincidentally build up the position framework as opposed to destroying it. There are requires a shift towards monetary models as opposed to standing contemplations to really address social and financial inconsistencies.

The idea of the "rich layer" has been a hostile issue. Pundits contend that barring monetarily well-off people from saved classifications is important to keep the advantages of reservations from arriving at the individuals who are now favored inside these gatherings. Nonetheless, others battle that monetary models alone may not catch the subtleties of authentic separation and social rejection.

The discussion likewise stretches out to the effect of reservations on meritocracy. Adversaries contend that the accentuation on position based reservations might think twice about nature of training and labor force, as applicants might be chosen in view of their rank as opposed to their capacities and capabilities. Finding some kind of harmony between tending to verifiable treacheries and guaranteeing meritocratic standards stays an imposing test.

Political Portrayal:

Past training and business, rank based reservations have been reached out to political portrayal to guarantee the consideration of underestimated networks in dynamic cycles. Saved seats for SCs and STs in nearby bodies, regulative gatherings, and Parliament plan to address authentic underrepresentation and enable these networks strategically.

While political reservations have prompted expanded portrayal, there are difficulties connected with the successful cooperation and strengthening of chosen agents. Issues like the propagation of hypocrisy, restricted admittance to assets, and the requirement for extensive improvement strategies in saved supporters are regions that expect thoughtfulness regarding guarantee that political reservations convert into significant change.

Diversity and Comprehensive Approaches:

The idea of diversity has acquired conspicuousness in conversations about reservations, underscoring the interconnected idea of different characters and types of separation. Perceiving that people might encounter various types of burden in view of the convergence of their standing, orientation, and monetary status has prompted a more nuanced and comprehensive comprehension of variety.

Endeavors are in progress to address the intricacies of multifacetedness and guarantee that booking approaches are receptive to the assorted necessities of people from minimized networks. This incorporates conversations about widening the models for reservations to include financial status and different elements that add to social impediment.

The Way Forward:

As India explores the intricate territory of station based reservations, the street ahead requires a nuanced and thorough methodology. Addressing the moves and reactions requires a guarantee to civil rights and inclusivity. Policymakers, researchers, and activists keep on investigating imaginative arrangements that go past the twofold of station and monetary models to make a more fair society.

Endeavors to find some kind of harmony between governmental policy regarding minorities in society and meritocracy are fundamental. This includes refining existing reservation strategies, investigating elective rules for incorporation, and tending to the underlying drivers of imbalance. A more comprehensive methodology that considers monetary, instructive, and social aspects is pivotal for the proceeded with pertinence and viability of rank based reservations.

Besides, cultivating a culture of inclusivity and separating station based biases is a necessary piece of the excursion toward civil rights. Schooling and mindfulness crusades that challenge generalizations and elevate understanding can add to destroying the well established social pecking orders that endure in Indian culture.

2. Impact on social dynamics

Rank based reservations, inserted inside India's governmental policy regarding minorities in society strategies, have used a significant impact on the country's social elements. These strategies, intended to amend verifiable shameful acts and elevate minimized networks, have made a permanent imprint on training, business, and political portrayal.

This investigation digs into the diverse effect of rank put together reservations with respect to social elements, dissecting both the positive changes and the nuanced challenges that have arisen directly following these governmental policy regarding minorities in society measures.

Change in Instructive Scene:
One of the main effects of position based reservations has been the extraordinary change in the instructive scene of India. By saving seats in instructive organizations for Booked Stations (SCs), Planned Clans (STs), and Other In reverse Classes (OBCs), the arrangements looked to destroy boundaries to schooling that generally underestimated networks confronted.

The positive effect is clear in the expanded enlistment of understudies from these networks in advanced education foundations. Admittance to schooling has engaged people who, for ages, were denied section into scholarly spaces. The strategy has led to another age of experts, breaking the shackles of intergenerational impediment.

Nonetheless, the effect isn't uniform across all disciplines and instructive levels. Concerns wait about the grouping of reservations in unambiguous fields and the underrepresentation of underestimated networks in regions like science and innovation. This features the requirement for a more nuanced approach that tends to the assorted desires and possibilities of people from various foundations.

Strengthening through Business Open doors:
Station based reservations in government occupations play had a urgent impact in making roads for monetary upliftment and strengthening. By saving an extent of government positions for SCs, STs, and OBCs, the strategies plan to guarantee that the public area labor force mirrors the variety of the populace.

The positive effect of reservations on work is obvious in the expanded portrayal of people from generally minimized networks in government workplaces. Admittance to stable government occupations, frequently joined by advantages and professional stability, has added to the financial progression of families, breaking the pattern of neediness.

Notwithstanding, challenges continue, especially concerning the underrepresentation of specific gatherings inside the saved classifications. The idea of the "smooth layer" was acquainted with address this issue by barring financially well-off people inside saved classes from the advantages of reservations. Finding some kind of harmony among inclusivity and forestalling unjustifiable benefit inside underestimated bunches stays a mind boggling task.

Political Strengthening and Portrayal:

Rank based reservations have reached out to the political field, planning to guarantee the consideration of minimized networks in dynamic cycles.

Held seats for SCs and STs in neighborhood bodies, official gatherings, and Parliament have tried to address verifiable underrepresentation and enable these networks strategically.

The positive effect of political reservations is apparent in the expanded portrayal of people from SCs and STs in chosen workplaces. Political strengthening has given a stage to minimized voices as well as affected strategy choices that straightforwardly influence these networks.

Nonetheless, challenges exist in guaranteeing that political reservations convert into significant change. Issues like the propagation of posturing, restricted admittance to assets, and the requirement for thorough improvement strategies in held electorates highlight the requirement for a more all encompassing way to deal with political strengthening.

Difficulties to Meritocracy and Quality:

One of the persevering through discusses encompassing standing based reservations rotates around the possible difficulties to meritocracy. Pundits contend that stressing rank based reservations might think twice about nature of instruction and the labor force, as up-and-comers might be chosen in view of their station as opposed to their capacities and capabilities.

While reservations intend to address verifiable treacheries, finding some kind of harmony among inclusivity and meritocracy is fundamental. The booking strategies have gone through legitimate investigation, with the High Court forcing a cap of half on reservations and underscoring that monetary measures alone can't be the reason for reservations.

Finding some kind of harmony is a continuous test. Guaranteeing that legitimacy isn't forfeited while tending to verifiable differences requires cautious execution, constant assessment, and a pledge to refining strategies in light of developing necessities and conditions.

Propagation of Rank Characters:

Rank based reservations have been dependent upon analysis for possibly propagating position characters instead of destroying the standing framework. Pundits contend that by zeroing in on station based reservations, the strategies coincidentally build up the social order as opposed to cultivating social joining.

Endeavors to address this worry incorporate requires a shift towards financial measures instead of standing contemplations. Some contend that monetary drawback, regardless of station, ought to be the essential model for governmental policy regarding minorities in society strategies to guarantee a more comprehensive methodology.

Adjusting the need to correct verifiable treacheries with the basic to cultivate a general public that rises above station differentiations stays a complex cultural test. The nuanced idea of India's social texture requires continuous discourse and versatile arrangement measures to explore the complexities of station elements.

Diversity and Comprehensive Approaches:

The idea of diversity, recognizing the interconnected idea of different personalities and types of segregation, has acquired conspicuousness in conversations about reservations. Perceiving that people might encounter different types of inconvenience in view of the crossing point of their standing, orientation, and financial status has prompted a more nuanced and comprehensive comprehension of variety.

Endeavors are in progress to address the intricacies of multifacetedness inside reservation arrangements. This incorporates conversations about expanding the measures for reservations to include monetary status and different variables that add to social drawback.

Inclusivity that considers the different encounters of people from underestimated networks is critical for the proceeded with pertinence and viability of position based reservations. This approach mirrors a comprehension that civil rights requires arrangements that go past parallel differentiations and record for the complicated interchange of characters.

Financial Inconsistencies and Financial Portability:

Standing based reservations have contributed altogether to tending to financial inconsistencies by giving open doors to financial versatility. Admittance to schooling and government occupations has been instrumental in breaking the pattern of neediness and encouraging financial strengthening inside generally underestimated networks.

The positive effect on monetary inconsistencies, notwithstanding, is dependent upon resolving more extensive underlying issues like admittance to quality essential and optional instruction, medical care, and financial open doors. Station based reservations, while groundbreaking, are one part of a more extensive procedure expected to handle the main drivers of imbalance.

Endeavors to advance business, expertise improvement, and comprehensive monetary arrangements are fundamental for guaranteeing that the advantages of reservations stretch out past government occupations and instructive organizations. Extensive measures that address the all encompassing necessities of people from minimized networks are fundamental to maintainable financial versatility.

Social Agreement and Incorporation:

Station based reservations have added to encouraging social concordance by tending to verifiable complaints and making pathways for joining. The strategies connote a promise to building a comprehensive society where people from different foundations have equivalent chances to flourish.

Notwithstanding, difficulties to social agreement continue, especially in settings where reservations are seen as leaning toward specific networks over others. Discoursed that underline the common objectives of balance, civil rights, and financial improvement are significant for cultivating understanding and solidarity.

Endeavors to advance social amicability reach out past strategies to envelop instructive educational plans, social drives, and local area commitment programs. Drives that feature shared chronicles, normal desires, and aggregate advancement add to building a more durable and incorporated society.

2.2 The need for gender-based reservations

Orientation based reservations, a type of governmental policy regarding minorities in society, have arisen as a pivotal system to address well established orientation disparities and engage ladies in different areas of public life. With regards to India, where verifiable and social elements have added to unavoidable orientation inconsistencies, the call for orientation based reservations has picked up speed as a way to correct verifiable treacheries and make a more comprehensive and fair society. This investigation dives into the convincing requirement for orientation based reservations, analyzing the verifiable setting of orientation disparity in India, the determined difficulties ladies face, and the possible effect of governmental policy regarding minorities in society in encouraging ladies' strengthening.

Verifiable Setting of Orientation Disparity in India:

The verifiable setting of orientation disparity in India is profoundly entwined with social, social, and financial elements. Conventional standards and man centric designs have propagated orientation jobs that frequently limit ladies' chances and admittance to assets. Regardless of progress in different spaces, orientation abberations endure in regions like training, business, and political portrayal.

By and large, ladies in India have confronted obstructions in getting to schooling, with lower education rates contrasted with men. The labor force has frequently been set apart by orientation based isolation, with ladies lopsidedly packed in low-paying and casual areas. Also, ladies' political portrayal has been restricted, reflecting more extensive cultural perspectives that minimize their part in dynamic cycles.

Challenges Ladies Face:

While steps have been made in propelling ladies' freedoms, huge difficulties persevere, ruining the acknowledgment of orientation correspondence in India. One of the significant difficulties is the pervasiveness of orientation based savagery, including aggressive behavior at home, lewd behavior, and illegal exploitation. The feeling of dread toward savagery limits ladies' versatility and cooperation in broad daylight spaces.

As far as schooling, there are still abberations in enlistment and culmination rates, especially in provincial regions. Financial abberations additionally persevere, with ladies confronting wage holes and restricted admittance to formal work potential open doors. Besides, social standards and predispositions add to the underrepresentation of ladies in administrative roles, both in the general population and confidential areas.

The weight of neglected homegrown work stays a critical obstacle to ladies' expert progression. Customary assumptions frequently bind ladies to providing care jobs, restricting their capacity to take part completely in monetary and social exercises. This complex arrangement of difficulties highlights the requirement for complete and designated intercessions to really address orientation imbalances.

The Criticalness of Orientation Based Reservations:

Against this setting of tenacious difficulties, the desperation for orientation based reservations becomes obvious. Governmental policy regarding minorities in society, as exemplified by orientation based reservations, is a proactive technique to counter verifiable hindrances and set out open doors for ladies to take part completely in different circles of public life.

Instructive Strengthening:

Orientation based reservations in instructive foundations can act as an impetus for instructive strengthening. By saving seats for ladies, particularly in advanced education, this approach expects to connect the orientation hole in instructive achievement. Expanded portrayal of ladies in scholastic settings encourages a different learning climate as well as difficulties generalizations and customary assumptions.

The effect of instructive strengthening reaches out past individual ladies to the more extensive local area. Instructed ladies are bound to add to the financial advancement of their families and networks. Besides, they assume a vital part in breaking intergenerational patterns of neediness and detriment.

Improving Financial Open doors:

Orientation based reservations in business are instrumental in tending to the long-standing financial differences looked by ladies. By holding positions in people in general and confidential areas, this arrangement tries to destroy obstructions to ladies' entrance into the conventional labor force. This, thus, adds to financial strengthening, restricting compensation holes, and giving ladies roads for proficient development.

The financial strengthening of ladies benefits people as well as meaningfully affects society. Expanded monetary freedom for ladies can prompt better generally speaking family prosperity and a decrease in orientation based financial variations.

Political Portrayal:

Orientation based reservations in political circles are pivotal for guaranteeing that ladies have a significant voice in the dynamic cycles that shape their lives. By holding seats in nearby bodies, regulative gatherings, and Parliament, this arrangement looks to address the authentic underrepresentation of ladies in legislative issues.

Political portrayal isn't just about numbers; it is tied in with enhancing different viewpoints and needs. Ladies in positions of authority can advocate for strategies that address orientation based savagery, advance ladies' freedoms, and establish an empowering climate for the full acknowledgment of ladies' true capacity.

Changing Cultural Discernments:

Orientation based reservations assume an essential part in testing and changing cultural discernments with respect to ladies' capacities and jobs. By effectively advancing the support of ladies in instructive, proficient, and political circles, these strategies send a strong message about the worth of orientation uniformity.

Changing cultural insights is a progressive cycle, and governmental policy regarding minorities in society fills in as an unmistakable and noticeable move toward destroying generalizations. Expanded perceivability of ladies in different jobs adds to a social shift, cultivating a climate where ladies are perceived and regarded for their abilities, gifts, and authority capacities.

Tending to Multifacetedness:

Orientation based reservations, when carried out nicely, can likewise address multifacetedness — the interconnected idea of different characters and types of segregation. Strategies that consider the convergence of orientation with different factors like station, class, and identity guarantee a more comprehensive way to deal with governmental policy regarding minorities in society.

Perceiving the assorted encounters of ladies from various foundations is fundamental for making arrangements that reverberate with the lived real factors, everything being equal. An interconnected methodology guarantees that the advantages of reservations arrive at the people who face numerous types of burden.

Expected Effect of Orientation Based Reservations:

The expected effect of orientation based reservations reaches out past the singular level to cultural and foundational change. Here are key regions where governmental policy regarding minorities in society can achieve significant change:

Breaking the Biased based impediment:

Orientation based reservations make ready for ladies to break the supposed unfair limitation in different areas.

Whether in corporate meeting rooms, logical exploration, or political fields, reservations give a system to destroy underlying hindrances that have generally restricted ladies' vertical versatility.

The presence of ladies in administrative roles fills in as a strong image, rousing people in the future of ladies to seek to and accomplish positions of authority in different fields.

Cultivating Comprehensive Strategies:

The consideration of ladies in dynamic cycles through orientation based reservations adds to the definition of additional comprehensive strategies. Ladies pioneers offer interesting viewpoints and needs of real value, guaranteeing that arrangements address the assorted requirements of the whole populace.

In governmental issues, for instance, ladies pioneers have been instrumental in pushing for regulation connected with conceptive freedoms, orientation based savagery, and ladies' wellbeing — regions that might have been disregarded without their dynamic association.

Social and Attitudinal Movements:

Orientation based reservations can add to more extensive social and attitudinal movements in regards to the jobs and abilities of ladies. At the point when ladies possess positions generally overwhelmed by men, it challenges assumptions about orientation jobs and abilities.

Such changes in perspectives are fundamental for destroying imbued generalizations that propagate orientation disparity. Openness to ladies in different jobs advances a more broad and comprehensive comprehension of what ladies can accomplish.

Building Good examples:

Governmental policy regarding minorities in society sets out open doors for ladies to become noticeable good examples in different fields. At the point when little kids see ladies succeeding in schooling, vocations, and administrative roles, they are bound to imagine comparative opportunities for themselves.

Building a pipeline of ladies good examples is significant for rousing the up and coming age of ladies to try to and accomplish their maximum capacity. This, thusly, adds to the standardization of ladies' presence in spaces generally overwhelmed by men.

Guaranteeing Reasonable Turn of events:

Orientation equity is complicatedly connected to supportable turn of events. At the point when ladies have equivalent admittance to schooling, work, and political interest, the general prosperity of social orders gets to the next level. Concentrates reliably show that enabling ladies emphatically affects wellbeing results, instruction levels, and financial turn of events.

Orientation based reservations, by tending to verifiable disservices, add to making a more impartial and economical society. The advantages stretch out past individual strengthening to cultural advancement and improvement.

Counterarguments and Discussions:

While the requirement for orientation based reservations is convincing, it is critical to recognize counterarguments and take part in valuable discussions. A few normal worries and reactions include:

Meritocracy versus Portrayal:

A repetitive discussion spins around the pressure among meritocracy and the requirement for portrayal. Pundits contend that reservations might think twice about standards by focusing on character over capabilities.

Finding some kind of harmony between guaranteeing portrayal and keeping up with meritocratic guidelines is a perplexing test. Straightforward and comprehensive choice cycles, combined with designated intercessions to address foundational obstructions, can assist with alleviating these worries.

Diversity and Inclusivity:

Orientation based reservations, on the off chance that not carried out with a multifaceted focal point, may coincidentally avoid ladies confronting numerous types of impediment. A strategy that exclusively centers around orientation disregarding variables like station, class, and nationality may not address the different requirements, everything being equal.

Arrangements lie in making strategies that embrace diversity and guarantee inclusivity. Considering the remarkable difficulties looked by ladies from changed foundations is fundamental for setting out impartial open doors.

Long haul Effect versus Momentary Additions:

Pundits contend that while orientation based reservations might yield momentary additions in portrayal, they probably won't address the underlying drivers of orientation imbalance. Long haul influence requires complete measures that address foundational issues, including social standards, inclinations, and cultural perspectives.

Orientation based reservations ought to be seen as a feature of a more extensive procedure as opposed to an independent arrangement. Corresponding measures, for example, instructive changes, mindfulness crusades, and authoritative changes, are vital for supported progress.

Execution Difficulties:

The successful execution of orientation based reservations presents down to earth difficulties. Guaranteeing that saved positions are filled by qualified and fit people, forestalling posturing, and exploring social obstruction are critical obstacles.

Hearty execution components, including observing and assessment systems, are urgent for the outcome of orientation based reservations. Cooperative endeavors including government offices, common society, and the confidential area can add to beating execution challenges.

1. **Historical context**

   To fathom the squeezing need for orientation based reservations in India, it is basic to dig into the authentic setting that has molded and propagated orientation disparities in the country. India, a land saturated with rich social and verifiable embroidery, has likewise been set apart by profoundly instilled male centric standards, inflexible orientation jobs, and fundamental oppression ladies. This verifiable background establishes the groundwork for understanding the underlying foundations of orientation based governmental policy regarding minorities in society and the basic to amend exceptionally old shameful acts.

   Old Cultural Designs:

   The foundations of orientation imbalance in India can be followed back to antiquated cultural designs and strict texts that arranged orientation jobs. Vedic writing, while at the same time containing philosophical and scholarly fortunes, frequently reflected winning male centric standards. The Manusmriti, an old legitimate text, organized the subjection of ladies, recommending severe sets of principles that consigned them to subordinate jobs inside the family and society. In this authentic setting, ladies were in many cases denied admittance to schooling and were bound to homegrown jobs. The overall standards propagated a progressive construction that set men at the pinnacle of cultural request, further digging in orientation based separation.

Middle age Period:

The middle age time frame in India saw the rise of different traditions and realms, each adding to the molding of cultural standards. While certain ladies in sovereignty appreciated, influential places, most of ladies confronted foundational oppression. The prohibitive acts of purdah (confinement of ladies) and sati (widow immolation) were common, mirroring the well established orientation predispositions that saturated society.

The socio-strict changes started during the English frontier time frame achieved a few changes, including regulations to boycott sati and advance widow remarriage. In any case, these changes were many times restricted in their effect, and conventional standards kept on affecting cultural perspectives toward ladies.

Frontier Impact:

The English frontier time frame in India, spreading over almost two centuries, impressively affected orientation relations. While provincial rule saw endeavors to resolve specific social issues, including kid marriage and widowhood, it additionally sustained man centric standards through its legitimate and authoritative designs.

The presentation of English schooling, essentially focused on at men, made an instructive orientation hole that persevered for ages. The provincial overall set of laws frequently worked inside the structure of existing man centric standards, and ladies' privileges were optional to pilgrim regulatory needs.

Post-Autonomy Period:

India's excursion toward freedom in 1947 denoted a huge defining moment, offering a chance to reconsider cultural standards and usher in moderate changes. The composers of the Indian Constitution, perceiving the requirement for orientation balance, revered principal freedoms that dependable equivalent assurance and non-separation.

Notwithstanding, the post-autonomy time additionally uncovered the tirelessness of orientation based segregation. Cultural perspectives, profoundly imbued over hundreds of years, kept on molding the status and open doors accessible to ladies. The battle for ladies' freedoms picked up speed, with spearheading figures like Rukmini Devi Arundale, Kamaladevi Chattopadhyay, and Sarojini Naidu pushing for orientation balance.

Rise of Governmental policy regarding minorities in society:

The acknowledgment that administrative measures were crucial for address settled in orientation variations prompted the development of governmental policy regarding minorities in society arrangements. The presentation of bookings for ladies in nearby administration, known as Panchayati Raj organizations, in the mid 1990s was a turning point. This noticeable a conscious work to guarantee ladies' portrayal in dynamic bodies at the grassroots level.

The Ladies' Booking Bill, proposed in the Indian Parliament in the mid 2000s, meant to stretch out comparable reservations to the public and state councils. In any case, notwithstanding rehashed endeavors, the bill has confronted huge difficulties in earning agreement and getting section.

Rank Based Reservations and Orientation:

India's involvement in rank based reservations offers experiences into the intricacies of governmental policy regarding minorities in society. While at first centered around addressing verifiable shameful acts connected with standing, the strategies accidentally highlighted the interconnection of segregation, including that in view of orientation. Standing based reservations, while groundbreaking, didn't necessarily in every case address the particular difficulties looked by ladies from minimized networks.

Perceiving this hole, there have been requires a more nuanced and comprehensive methodology that recognizes the one of a kind battles of ladies inside different position gatherings. This interconnected focal point stresses the requirement for governmental policy regarding minorities in society arrangements that address the multi-layered nature of separation, considering both orientation and rank elements.

Tenacious Orientation Abberations:

Regardless of regulative endeavors and gradual advancement, orientation differences continue across different circles in India. Instructive fulfillment stays lopsided, with rustic and underestimated networks confronting more noteworthy difficulties. The labor force keeps on being set apart by orientation based word related isolation, with ladies moved in lower-paying and casual areas.

Viciousness against ladies, both in private and public spaces, stays an unavoidable issue. Profoundly imbued male centric standards add to the propagation of oppressive works on, restricting ladies' independence and potential open doors for financial and social headway.

Effect of Globalization:

The powers of globalization, while adding to financial development and urbanization, have additionally had complex ramifications for orientation elements in India. While certain ladies have accessed new open doors, the advantages have not been consistently disseminated. The computerized orientation partition, for example, features abberations in ladies' admittance to innovation and advanced education.

Globalization has achieved changes in cultural mentalities, yet it has additionally presented ladies to new types of double-dealing and difficulties. The intricate exchange of customary standards and worldwide impacts highlights the requirement for designated governmental policy regarding minorities in society to address the particular weaknesses looked by ladies.

The Pressing Requirement for Orientation Based Reservations:

Notwithstanding this verifiable scenery set apart by relentless orientation disparities, the requirement for orientation based reservations in India becomes earnest and convincing. Governmental policy regarding minorities in society isn't only a reaction to contemporary difficulties yet is well established in the verifiable treacheries that have molded the situation with ladies in Indian culture.

Tending to Authentic Treacheries:

Orientation based reservations are a proactive reaction to address verifiable treacheries that have denied ladies equivalent open doors. By recognizing the foundational segregation implanted in cultural designs, governmental policy regarding minorities in society tries to redress lopsided characteristics that have continued for a really long time.

The reservations give a system to break the pattern of intergenerational weakness, guaranteeing that people in the future of ladies approach valuable open doors that were generally denied to their ancestors.

Encouraging Equivalent Portrayal:

The underrepresentation of ladies in different circles, be it training, work, or political initiative, is an unmistakable impression of verifiable predispositions. Orientation based reservations are an intentional and designated mediation to encourage equivalent portrayal and destroy boundaries that have restricted ladies' investment.

Equivalent portrayal isn't just about mathematical equality; it is tied in with guaranteeing that ladies have a significant voice in dynamic cycles that shape strategies and establishments. This inclusivity adds to additional hearty and evenhanded results.

Testing Generalizations and Standards:

Governmental policy regarding minorities in society challenges profoundly imbued generalizations and standards that have consigned ladies to predefined jobs. By effectively advancing ladies' cooperation in areas generally overwhelmed by men, these strategies send a strong message that difficulties assumptions about ladies' capacities.

The effect goes past the singular ladies who benefit from reservations; it adds to moving cultural mentalities and cultivating a culture where ladies are perceived for their abilities, gifts, and initiative potential.

Making Pathways for Strengthening:

Governmental policy regarding minorities in society makes unmistakable pathways for the strengthening of ladies. Whether through expanded admittance to training, financial open doors, or political administration, these arrangements are instrumental in destroying boundaries that frustrate ladies' independence and office.

The strengthening of ladies affects families, networks, and society at large. At the point when ladies are enabled, they add to the financial advancement of their networks, breaking the pattern of destitution and disparity.

Guaranteeing Multifaceted Inclusivity:

A fundamental part of orientation based reservations is the acknowledgment of diversity — the interconnected idea of different personalities and types of separation. Governmental policy regarding minorities in society that thinks about orientation as well as elements like standing, class, and nationality guarantees a more comprehensive methodology.

Perceiving the assorted encounters of ladies from various foundations is fundamental for making arrangements that reverberate with the lived real factors, everything being equal. An interconnected focal point adds to evenhanded open doors that address the mind boggling interchange of characters.

Counterarguments and Difficulties:

While the requirement for orientation based reservations is convincing, it is urgent to recognize and draw in with counterarguments and difficulties that these strategies might present.

Meritocracy versus Portrayal:

One normal analysis spins around the pressure among meritocracy and the requirement for portrayal. Pundits contend that reservations might think twice about standards by focusing on personality over capabilities.

Finding some kind of harmony between guaranteeing portrayal and keeping up with meritocratic principles is an intricate test. Straightforward and comprehensive choice cycles, combined with designated intercessions to address fundamental boundaries, can assist with alleviating these worries.

Cultural Attitudinal Movements:

Governmental policy regarding minorities in society can add to changing cultural mentalities, however it can't be a panacea for well established social standards and predispositions. Moving cultural mentalities requires thorough endeavors past regulative measures.

Taking part in social and instructive drives that challenge orientation generalizations, advancing orientation touchy educational programs, and encouraging exchanges about orientation equity are fundamental parts of a comprehensive methodology.

Execution Difficulties:

The successful execution of orientation based reservations presents viable difficulties. Guaranteeing that saved positions are filled by qualified and proficient people, forestalling posturing, and exploring social opposition are huge obstacles.

Powerful execution instruments, including observing and assessment systems, are essential for the progress of orientation based reservations. Cooperative endeavors including government organizations, common society, and the confidential area can add to beating execution challenges.

Interconnection and Inclusivity:

Orientation based reservations, in the event that not carried out with a multifaceted focal point, may coincidentally prohibit ladies confronting different types of weakness. A strategy that exclusively centers around orientation disregarding variables like standing, class, and identity may not address the different necessities, everything being equal.

Arrangements lie in making approaches that embrace diversity and guarantee inclusivity. Considering the remarkable difficulties looked by ladies from changed foundations is fundamental for setting out fair open doors.

Long haul Effect versus Transient Additions:

Pundits contend that while orientation based reservations might yield transient additions in portrayal, they probably won't address the main drivers of orientation imbalance.

Long haul influence requires exhaustive measures that address fundamental issues, including social standards, inclinations, and cultural mentalities.

Orientation based reservations ought to be seen as a feature of a more extensive methodology instead of an independent arrangement. Correlative measures, for example, instructive changes, mindfulness crusades, and administrative changes, are essential for supported progress.

2. **Global precedents**

The basic of orientation balance is a worldwide test that rises above boundaries, societies, and financial settings. Governmental policy regarding minorities in society, especially orientation based reservations, has been carried out in different structures across the globe as a way to address verifiable treacheries, redress orientation variations, and enable ladies. Inspecting worldwide points of reference gives significant experiences into the assorted methodologies, victories, and difficulties related with governmental policy regarding minorities in society drives. From Nordic nations to Latin America and then some, these points of reference offer illustrations that can illuminate and shape viable methodologies for ladies' strengthening in India.

Nordic Nations:

Nordic nations, including Sweden, Norway, Denmark, Finland, and Iceland, are many times refered to as worldwide forerunners in orientation equity. These countries have executed governmental policy regarding minorities in society measures to advance ladies' portrayal in different circles, showing the way that proactive arrangements can add to significant advancement.

Political Portrayal:

Nordic nations have supported orientation quantities in political portrayal as a way to address the underrepresentation of ladies in chosen workplaces. Norway, for instance, carried out a compulsory 40% orientation portion for corporate sheets in 2006. This approach has altogether expanded the quantity of ladies serving on sheets, showing the adequacy of governmental policy regarding minorities in society in testing orientation lopsided characteristics in administrative roles.

Examples for India: Nordic nations' encounters highlight the effect of setting clear and aggressive orientation quantities in political portrayal. India can draw motivation from these points of reference to plan and execute quantities that guarantee significant portrayal of ladies in authoritative bodies at all levels.

Working environment Equity:

Governmental policy regarding minorities in society in Nordic nations stretches out to the work environment, where endeavors to address orientation based word related isolation and advance variety are clear. These countries have carried out strategies to guarantee pay value, parental leave, and adaptable work game plans, adding to a more impartial workplace.

Illustrations for India: Tending to work environment disparities requires a far reaching approach that incorporates reservations as well as strong strategies that encourage an orientation comprehensive working environment. Gaining from Nordic nations, India can investigate drives that advance compensation straightforwardness, adaptable work game plans, and equivalent oper. doors for professional success.

Instructive Fairness:

Nordic nations have focused on orientation fairness in training, guaranteeing equivalent access and open doors for young men and young ladies. Endeavors to challenge orientation generalizations in instructive decisions and offer help for female understudies in science and innovation fields epitomize their obligation to separating conventional obstructions.

Examples for India: Training is an important landmark for orientation balance. India can profit from Nordic ways to deal with challenge orientation generalizations in training, urge young ladies to seek after modern fields, and offer designated help to address variations in instructive achievement.

Latin America:

Latin American nations have wrestled with authentic orientation abberations, and governmental policy regarding minorities in society measures have been executed to review these awkward nature. The district has seen striking advancement in political portrayal and legitimate systems to address orientation based viciousness.

Political Portrayal:

Nations like Argentina, Bolivia, and Ecuador have executed orientation shares to build ladies' portrayal in governmental issues. Argentina, for example, ordered a regulation in 1991 laying out a standard framework, adding to a huge expansion in the quantity of ladies serving in authoritative positions.

Examples for India: The Latin American experience exhibits the groundbreaking capability of orientation portions in governmental issues. India can draw motivation from these guides to create and implement standards that guarantee ladies' significant support in chosen workplaces.

Lawful Structures Against Orientation Based Savagery:

A few Latin American nations have carried out governmental policy regarding minorities in society through lawful structures to address orientation based brutality.

Regulations and strategies pointed toward forestalling and punishing savagery against ladies, including femicide, feature a promise to establishing a more secure climate for ladies.

Illustrations for India: Reinforcing lawful structures and executing proactive approaches to battle orientation based brutality is significant. India can gain from Latin American encounters to establish and uphold regulations that give vigorous insurance and backing to casualties of orientation based savagery.

Financial Strengthening:

Governmental policy regarding minorities in society in Latin America stretches out to monetary strengthening, with programs designated at tending to financial variations looked by ladies. Microfinance drives and backing for ladies business visionaries mean to improve monetary open doors and monetary autonomy.

Examples for India: Financial strengthening is a critical mainstay of orientation balance. India can investigate and adjust effective financial strengthening drives from Latin America to address the remarkable difficulties looked by ladies in getting to monetary open doors.

US:

The US has a long history of wrestling with issues of racial and orientation disparity. Governmental policy regarding minorities in society, albeit questionable, has been utilized to address verifiable treacheries and advance variety and consideration.

Advanced education:

Governmental policy regarding minorities in society in advanced education in the US has been a subject of broad discussion and legitimate difficulties. Strategies, for example, race-cognizant confirmations expect to increment variety in instructive foundations, including colleges and expert schools.

Examples for India: India can inspect the U.S. experience in governmental policy regarding minorities in society in advanced education to illuminate strategies that address differences in access and portrayal, guaranteeing variety and consideration in scholarly settings.

Corporate Variety Drives:

In the corporate area, variety drives in the US incorporate endeavors to expand portrayal of ladies and minorities in administrative roles. Organizations frequently set targets and carry out strategies to advance variety, value, and consideration.

Examples for India: Corporate variety drives give a model to tending to orientation differences in the confidential area. India can gain from the U.S. corporate area's way to deal with executing arrangements and practices that encourage orientation variety and consideration in positions of authority.

Legitimate Securities:

Governmental policy regarding minorities in society in the US incorporates legitimate securities against working environment separation in view of orientation and other safeguarded attributes. Regulation, for example, Title VII of the Social equality

Act restricts segregation and urges managers to embrace governmental policy regarding minorities in society measures.

Examples for India: Vigorous lawful securities are fundamental for tending to orientation separation in the working environment. India can draw from the U.S. experience to fortify and uphold regulation that guarantees equivalent open doors and securities against orientation based segregation.

South Africa:

South Africa's set of experiences of politically-sanctioned racial segregation and racial separation has formed its way to deal with governmental policy regarding minorities in society, known as Dark Financial Strengthening (Honey bee). Honey bee approaches expect to address verifiable lopsided characteristics by advancing monetary open doors for recently hindered gatherings, including ladies.

Monetary Strengthening:

Honey bee strategies in South Africa envelop monetary strengthening drives, including special acquisition, endeavor improvement, and abilities advancement. These strategies are intended to advance the consideration of ladies and generally minimized bunches in the monetary scene.

Examples for India: South Africa's Honey bee strategies offer bits of knowledge into the plan and execution of financial strengthening drives. India can investigate comparable ways to deal with address monetary differences looked by ladies, especially those from underestimated networks.

Political Portrayal:

South Africa has carried out governmental policy regarding minorities in society measures to advance political portrayal. The African Public Congress (ANC) has utilized standards to guarantee relative portrayal of ladies in regulative bodies.

Illustrations for India: Amounts for political portrayal have been successful in South Africa, and India can attract examples to figure out and carry out comparable arrangements that upgrade ladies' portrayal in political foundations.

Instructive Fairness:

Governmental policy regarding minorities in society in training in South Africa remembers measures to address verifiable differences for access and quality. Approaches, for example, particular admission to colleges mean to redress lopsided characteristics and guarantee equivalent open doors.

Illustrations for India: South Africa's way to deal with governmental policy regarding minorities in society in training gives a model to tending to verifiable drawbacks. India can investigate comparative approaches to upgrade instructive open doors and results for ladies.

Normal Subjects and Illustrations:

While assorted in their unique circumstances, these worldwide points of reference uncover normal subjects and examples that can illuminate India's way to deal with governmental policy regarding minorities in society for ladies' strengthening:

Clear and Aggressive Targets:

Effective governmental policy regarding minorities in society drives set clear and aggressive focuses for portrayal. Whether in governmental issues, training, or the corporate area, clear cut standards and targets give a guide to accomplishing significant orientation equity.

Lawful Securities and Authorization:

Solid lawful securities and authorization systems are fundamental for the progress of governmental policy regarding minorities in society. Lawful systems that deny orientation based segregation and give solutions for infringement add to establishing an empowering climate.

Multifaceted Methodologies:

Recognizing multifacetedness — taking into account the interconnected idea of different characters and types of separation — is essential. Effective drives perceive and address the remarkable difficulties looked by ladies from different foundations.

All encompassing and Extensive Techniques:

Governmental policy regarding minorities in society is best when carried out as a feature of an all encompassing and complete methodology. This incorporates tending to portrayal as well as monetary incongruities, instructive imbalances, and social standards that sustain orientation disparity.

Public Mindfulness and Backing:

Public mindfulness and backing assume a fundamental part in the progress of governmental policy regarding minorities in society drives. Drawing in with general society, testing generalizations, and encouraging a culture that values orientation correspondence add to the achievement and supportability of these strategies.

Difficulties and Reactions:

While worldwide points of reference offer significant bits of knowledge, it is pivotal to recognize difficulties and reactions related with governmental policy regarding minorities in society:

Obstruction and Kickback:

Governmental policy regarding minorities in society drives frequently face obstruction and reaction, with pundits contending that such strategies subvert meritocracy.

Public discernment and opposition can present huge difficulties to the effective execution of governmental policy regarding minorities in society.

Execution Difficulties:

The viable execution of governmental policy regarding minorities in society approaches requires vigorous systems, checking, and assessment. Challenges in carrying out quantities, guaranteeing consistence, and forestalling hypocrisy can hinder the progress of these drives.

Multifacetedness and Inclusivity:

While governmental policy regarding minorities in society means to address verifiable weaknesses, there is a gamble of neglecting diversity and neglecting to incorporate ladies confronting numerous types of disservice. Strategies should be planned in view of inclusivity, taking into account the different encounters, all things considered.

Long haul Effect versus Momentary Additions:

Governmental policy regarding minorities in society might yield transient additions in portrayal, however tending to the main drivers of orientation imbalance requires far reaching, long haul techniques. Offsetting transient increases with supported progress is a basic thought.

Chapter 3

Advocacy and the Birth of the Women's Reservation Bill

The backing for orientation fairness in Indian governmental issues has a celebrated history set apart by versatility, assurance, and an aggregate obligation to testing foundational obstructions. At the core of this development lies the Ladies' Booking Bill, a regulative drive that tries to address the glaring orientation uniqueness in political portrayal. The excursion from grassroots activism to parliamentary discussions mirrors the complex endeavors of backers, policymakers, and common society in pushing for governmental policy regarding minorities in society to engage ladies and change the political scene.

Verifiable Setting:
The require ladies' political portrayal picked up speed in the post-freedom time, with the outlining of the Indian Constitution in 1950. While the Constitution revered the standards of uniformity and non-segregation, the portrayal of ladies in chosen bodies remained excessively low. The underrepresentation of ladies in dynamic positions turned into a glaring hole that requested consideration and restorative measures.

In the many years that followed, different grassroots developments and ladies' associations started supporting for expanded political cooperation and portrayal. Spearheading figures like Rajkumari Amrit Kaur, Vijaya Lakshmi Pandit, and Sucheta Kripalani assumed urgent parts in establishing the groundwork for future promotion endeavors. Nonetheless, it was in the late twentieth century that the interest for administrative activity got momentum.

Development of the Ladies' Booking Bill:
The conventional excursion of the Ladies' Booking Bill started during the 1990s, with the presentation of the bill in the Indian Parliament. The essential target of the bill was to hold seats for ladies in the Lok Sabha (Place of Individuals) and state administrative gatherings. The proposed regulation planned to reserve a particular level of seats solely for ladies, guaranteeing their immediate and significant support in the political cycle.

The underlying rendition of the bill, ordinarily known as the 81st Sacred Change Bill, was presented in 1996 by the Unified Front government. Be that as it may, the bill confronted opposition and couldn't get the important agreement for section. Ensuing endeavors to once again introduce the bill confronted comparable difficulties, with discussions and conversations frequently mirroring a range of suppositions on the need and practicality of orientation based reservations.

Key Arrangements of the Bill:

The Ladies' Booking Bill, in its different cycles, proposed to save 33% of the all out seats in the Lok Sabha and state regulative congregations for ladies. The held seats were to be pivoted in various political race cycles, guaranteeing that various electorates profited from expanded ladies' portrayal over the long haul. The bill additionally included arrangements to save seats for ladies having a place with Planned Ranks (SC) and Booked Clans (ST) to address diverse imbalances.

The center reasoning behind the bill was to address the primary boundaries that impeded ladies' entrance into discretionary governmental issues. By reserving a critical level of seats, the bill planned to make a more comprehensive and impartial political scene, testing the profoundly dug in orientation predispositions that had restricted ladies' support in administration.

Grassroots Support and Common Society Preparation:

At the core of the support for the Ladies' Booking Bill is the preparation of common society associations, ladies' gatherings, and grassroots activists. The development picked up speed through deliberate endeavors to bring issues to light about the requirement for expanded ladies' portrayal and to earn support from assorted areas of society.

Ladies' Associations and Organizations:

Ladies' associations, both at the public and grassroots levels, assumed a crucial part in upholding for the bill.

These associations took part in mindfulness crusades, led examinations on the effect of ladies' portrayal, and activated help through gatherings, courses, and public discussions.

Associations like the All India Ladies' Meeting (AIWC), Public League of Indian Ladies (NFIW), and others effectively partook in the support endeavors. Their job stretched out past simple campaigning for official change; they went about as impetuses for a more extensive social discourse on orientation equity in legislative issues.

Mass Preparation and Missions:

Grassroots preparation was a sign of the backing effort for the Ladies' Booking Bill. Mass developments, rallies, and mark crusades were coordinated the nation over to fabricate public help. Ladies from assorted foundations, including country and underestimated networks, became vocal backers for the bill, sharing their accounts and stressing the groundbreaking capability of expanded portrayal.

Outstanding efforts, for example, the "1000 Ladies, 1000 Races" drive, looked to feature the critical requirement for ladies' voices in dynamic cycles. Grassroots preparation assumed a vital part in showing that the interest for the bill was not restricted to metropolitan or first class spaces however resounded with ladies across the social range.

Alliance Building and Partnerships:

Perceiving the significance of building unions, ladies' gatherings teamed up with other common society associations, scholastics, and moderate people to shape a considerable support alliance. These coalitions enhanced the message of orientation uniformity in governmental issues and worked with a more extensive way to deal with campaigning for the bill.

The Public Union for Ladies' Booking Bill (NAWRB) arose as a noticeable alliance upholding for the entry of the bill. This cooperative exertion united different voices and mastery to support the contention for governmental policy regarding minorities in society in political portrayal.

Parliamentary Discussions and Difficulties:

Notwithstanding the supported promotion and far and wide help for the Ladies' Booking Bill, its excursion through the Indian Parliament has been full of difficulties. The discussions inside parliamentary loads mirrored a scope of viewpoints, and the bill confronted resistance, on philosophical grounds, yet in addition because of functional worries and political estimations.

Resistance and Discussions:

The Ladies' Booking Bill confronted resistance from different quarters, with a contending that it could prompt hypocrisy or that it could think twice about in governmental issues. Concerns were raised about the expected effect on party elements and the opposition of laid out political pioneers to surrender their positions.

The parliamentary discussions were set apart by extraordinary conversations on the instruments of execution, the level of held seats, and the likely ramifications for ideological groups. While numerous parliamentarians voiced their help for orientation uniformity, the bill's excursion through the official interaction was delayed and quarrelsome.

Slowed down Progress and Slips by:

Regardless of numerous endeavors to pass the bill, progress was frequently slowed down because of an absence of agreement and the changing political scene. Slips in the regulative cycle, alongside shifts in political needs, added to a feeling of dissatisfaction among advocates and brought up issues about the responsibility of political pioneers to orientation correspondence.

The bill passed with the disintegration of each Lok Sabha, requiring its renewed introduction in resulting meetings. This example of omissions highlighted the requirement for supported and vital backing endeavors to defeat the obstacles looked by the bill.

Job of Political Authority:

The job of political authority in molding the fate of the Ladies' Booking Bill couldn't possibly be more significant. While a few political pioneers supported the reason for orientation equity and effectively upheld the bill, others had doubts or safe. The elements inside ideological groups, the impact of male centric standards, and discretionary estimations generally assumed a part in molding the position of political pioneers.

Bosses of Progress:

A few political pioneers arose as bosses of the Ladies' Booking Bill, upholding for its section both inside and outside the parliament. Pioneers like Pramod Mahajan, Sharad Yadav, and others assumed instrumental parts in building agreement and collecting support from their friends.

Ladies pioneers inside ideological groups, including Sonia Gandhi, Sushma Swaraj, and Mamata Banerjee, likewise loaned their voices to the reason. Their support exhibited that orientation equity was a ladies' issue as well as a common obligation that necessary the responsibility of pioneers across sexes.

Opposition and Irresoluteness:

Nonetheless, obstruction and indecision inside political circles persevered. A few chiefs communicated worries about the likely effect on the power elements inside parties, dreading unseen fits of turmoil or obstruction from male party individuals. The political analytics of keeping up with existing power structures frequently conflicted with the basic of destroying orientation hindrances.

The Ladies' Booking Bill became caught in the perplexing snare of political contemplations, where transient constituent gains and party elements overshadowed long haul responsibilities to orientation equity.

Popular Assessment and Discernment:

The backing for the Ladies' Booking Bill reached out past the passages of ability to impact popular assessment. While there was far reaching support for expanded ladies' portrayal, disparate perspectives on the particulars of the bill, including the level of held seats and the components of execution, featured the intricacy of public opinion.

Metropolitan Rustic Gap:

The metropolitan rustic gap assumed a part in forming general assessment on the Ladies' Booking Bill. While metropolitan focuses frequently saw more prominent mindfulness and vocal help for orientation fairness, rustic regions encountered a more changed reaction. Social standards, customary power structures, and differing levels of mindfulness about the bill added to different viewpoints.

Backing endeavors designated both metropolitan and country crowds, accentuating the groundbreaking effect of ladies' portrayal on administration and local area advancement.

Media Stories:

Media assumed a significant part in molding public stories around the Ladies' Booking Bill. Article assessments, news inclusion, and public discussions added to outlining the talk on orientation uniformity in legislative issues. The media filled in as a stage for promoters to explain their positions, share examples of overcoming adversity, and participate in banters with rivals of the bill.

Notwithstanding, media inclusion additionally mirrored the intricacies of popular assessment, with assorted voices and viewpoints affecting the more extensive talk.

Influence on State-Level Drives:

While the Ladies' Booking Bill confronted difficulties at the public level, a few states went to proactive lengths to build ladies' portrayal in neighborhood administration. The execution of orientation amounts in Panchayati Raj establishments, especially in states like Maharashtra and West Bengal, filled in as fruitful models that showed the positive effect of governmental policy regarding minorities in society.

Panchayati Raj and Neighborhood Administration:

The execution of orientation quantities in Panchayati Raj foundations denoted a huge move toward decentralized ladies' portrayal. States like Maharashtra and West Bengal saw positive results, with ladies pioneers effectively taking part in dynamic cycles at the grassroots level.

The progress of state-level drives highlighted the practicality and effect of orientation based reservations in legislative issues. Advocates highlighted these models as proof of the extraordinary potential that comparative measures could have at the public level.

Exhibiting Examples of overcoming adversity:

Examples of overcoming adversity from states that executed orientation portions filled in as amazing assets for advocates. Stories of ladies pioneers actually resolving neighborhood issues, further developing administration, and testing conventional power elements resounded with both policymakers and general society. These examples of overcoming adversity became essential to the support account, dispersing questions about the adequacy of orientation based reservations.

Difficulties and Counterarguments:

While the promotion for the Ladies' Booking Bill gathered far and wide help, it was not without difficulties and counterarguments. Tending to these worries turned into a fundamental piece of the backing system to assemble agreement and relieve fears related with governmental policy regarding minorities in society in legislative issues.

Posturing and Meritocracy:

One normal counterargument against the Ladies' Booking Bill spun around the feeling of dread toward hypocrisy — that ladies chose through held seats may be seen as placeholders as opposed to qualified delegates. Pundits contended that the bill could think twice about meritocratic standards of constituent governmental issues.

Advocates answered by stressing the skill and capacities of ladies pioneers and featuring that reservations were a way to beat fundamental obstructions instead of a think twice about merit.

Influence on Political Elements:

A few rivals of the bill communicated worries about its possible effect on political elements inside parties. The apprehension about struggles under the surface, opposition from male party individuals, and the apparent danger to existing power structures prompted obstruction from inside political circles.

Advocates countered these worries by highlighting the positive encounters of states that executed orientation amounts, contending that the incorporation of ladies improved political talk and added to more comprehensive and powerful administration.

Established Difficulties:

Established difficulties were raised in regards to the arrangement of seats in view of orientation. Pundits contended that such grouping should have been visible as unfair and tested the established standards of balance.

Advocates fought that the governmental policy regarding minorities in society proposed by the bill was a transitory and essential measure to correct verifiable irregular characteristics. They contended that the bill was steady with the more extensive protected objectives of balance and equity.

Need for Thorough Changes:

A few pundits recommended that as opposed to zeroing in exclusively on reservations, extensive changes were expected to resolve foundational issues inside the political scene. The contention was that a more extensive arrangement of changes, including political financing straightforwardness, electing changes, and mindfulness crusades, would add to a more comprehensive change.

Advocates recognized the requirement for exhaustive changes yet stressed that reservations were a pivotal and quick move toward address the unmistakable orientation difference in political portrayal.

Current Status and Future Possibilities:

As of the latest update, the Ladies' Booking Bill has not been authorized into regulation. In spite of different endeavors to get its entry, the bill has confronted difficulties, slips by, and moving political needs. The perplexing exchange of elements, including political computations, obstruction inside ideological groups, and differing general suppositions, has added to the delayed excursion of the bill.

Reestablished Promotion Endeavors:

Support for the Ladies' Booking Bill keeps on being a dynamic and developing development. Common society associations, ladies' gatherings, and activists stay focused on the reason, and restored endeavors are occasionally embraced to reignite public talk and gather speed for the bill.

Job of the Future:

The more youthful age, with its uplifted attention to civil rights issues, has effectively taken part in backing endeavors for orientation equity in legislative issues. Youth-drove developments, online entertainment missions, and mindfulness drives have added to keeping the issue alive in open cognizance.

Worldwide Points of view:

Worldwide points of view on orientation uniformity and governmental policy regarding minorities in society keep on impacting the talk. Gaining from worldwide points of reference, remembering fruitful models of orientation portions for different nations, adds to the refinement of promotion procedures and the outlining of the discussion.

3.1 Grassroots movements for women's rights

The historical backdrop of ladies' privileges has been set apart by an embroidery of grassroots developments that have arisen naturally, determined by the aggregate voices of ladies looking for fairness, equity, and strengthening. From suffragette developments to contemporary lobbies for orientation correspondence, grassroots drives play had a significant impact in testing foundational treacheries, affecting strategy changes, and reshaping cultural impression of ladies' jobs and privileges. This investigation dives into the authentic advancement, key highlights, and the groundbreaking effect of grassroots developments for ladies' privileges.

Authentic Roots:

The underlying foundations of grassroots developments for ladies' freedoms can be followed back to the nineteenth and mid twentieth hundreds of years when ladies started coordinating to challenge the common standards that confined their admittance to schooling, the option to cast a ballot, and support in open life. The suffragette development, especially in the US and Europe, remains as an original illustration of grassroots activism that tried to tie down ladies' on the whole correct to cast a ballot.

Suffragette Development:

The suffragette development picked up speed in the late nineteenth and mid twentieth hundreds of years, with ladies requesting the option to partake in equitable cycles. Activists like Susan B. Anthony and Emmeline Pankhurst prepared ladies through grassroots missions, fights, and common defiance to get casting a ballot rights.

The suffragettes confronted critical opposition, including captures, detainment, and public backfire. Nonetheless, their relentless grassroots endeavors made ready for the possible emancipation of ladies in numerous nations.

First Wave Women's liberation:

The principal wave of woman's rights, fundamentally from the late nineteenth 100 years to the mid twentieth hundred years, saw the rise of grassroots developments supporting for ladies' testimonial, instructive open doors, and lawful changes. Activists participated in grassroots getting sorted out, cognizance raising exercises, and the distribution of writing to challenge male centric standards and unfair regulations.

Grassroots drives during this period established the groundwork for ensuing floods of woman's rights and sowed the seeds for progressing battles for orientation fairness.

Key Elements of Grassroots Developments:

Grassroots developments for ladies' privileges share a few key elements that recognize them from hierarchical, institutional methodologies. These qualities highlight the natural idea of these developments and their capacity to resound with the lived encounters of ladies across assorted social, financial, and social settings.

Decentralized and Comprehensive:

Grassroots developments are innately decentralized, frequently rising up out of nearby networks and including different members. They focus on inclusivity, inviting ladies from different foundations, encounters, and characters. This inclusivity fortifies the development's ability to address interconnected difficulties looked by ladies, taking into account factors like race, class, and sexual direction.

Base Up Preparation:

Grassroots developments are described by base up assembly, where the catalyst for change comes from the local area level as opposed to being forced from a higher place. Nearby activists and coordinators assume a vital part in preparing networks, cultivating fortitude, and making networks that enhance the aggregate voice of ladies.

Local area Commitment:

Local area commitment is a sign of grassroots developments. Activists frequently work straightforwardly inside networks, taking part in discourse, leading studios, and resolving nearby issues that reverberate with ladies' regular routines. This people group driven approach guarantees that the development is receptive to the exceptional difficulties looked by ladies in changed settings.

Strengthening and Expertise Building:

Grassroots developments focus on the strengthening of ladies not just as a way to accomplish strategy changes yet additionally as an end in itself. Expertise building drives, initiative preparation, and instructive projects are basic parts of these developments, expecting to improve ladies' organization, certainty, and ability to advocate for their privileges.

Multifacetedness:

A multifaceted methodology is vital to grassroots developments, recognizing the interconnected idea of different types of segregation. Activists perceive that ladies' encounters are molded by an intricate exchange of variables, including race, class, nationality, and sexuality. By embracing a multifaceted focal point, grassroots developments intend to address the remarkable difficulties looked by changed gatherings of ladies.

Direct Activity and Backing:

Grassroots developments are described by direct activity and backing. Whether through fights, walks, or missions, activists take part in noticeable and unmistakable endeavors to achieve change. This immediate commitment serves as a type of obstruction as well as a way to bring issues to light and gather speed for more extensive social change.

Contemporary Grassroots Developments:

While authentic developments laid the basis, contemporary grassroots developments for ladies' freedoms keep on advancing, answering new provokes and utilizing imaginative techniques to propel orientation uniformity.

#MeToo Development:

The #MeToo development, which acquired noticeable quality in the last part of the 2010s, is a strong illustration of contemporary grassroots activism. Starting from individual exposures of inappropriate behavior and attack, the development immediately spread universally, with ladies sharing their encounters across different ventures.

The #MeToo development depends via online entertainment stages for enhancement, empowering survivors to end the quietness and consider culprits responsible. Its decentralized nature considers the aggregate sharing of stories, making a virtual grassroots development that rises above geological limits.

Worldwide Ladies' Walks:

The Ladies' Walks that occurred around the world in the consequence of the 2016 U.S. official political race embody the strength of grassroots assembly. A large number of ladies and partners took part in walks, pushing for ladies' privileges, racial equity, LGBTQ+ freedoms, and natural equity.

These walks, coordinated at the neighborhood level and associated through a common vision, displayed the force of decentralized grassroots developments to join different voices under a typical reason.

Regenerative Freedoms Support:

Grassroots developments upholding for conceptive privileges have acquired unmistakable quality, especially in settings where admittance to regenerative medical care is under danger. Activists work at the local area level to challenge prohibitive strategies, bring issues to light about regenerative freedoms, and offer help for those confronting obstructions to conceptive medical services.

The diverse idea of these developments is apparent, as activists perceive that limitations on conceptive privileges lopsidedly influence underestimated networks.

Extraordinary Effect:

Grassroots developments for ladies' freedoms have achieved groundbreaking changes, in authoritative and strategy spaces as well as in cultural mentalities and view of orientation jobs.

Authoritative Changes:

Verifiable and contemporary grassroots developments have added to huge official changes that perceive and safeguard ladies' freedoms. The suffragette development, for instance, prompted the giving of casting a ballot rights for ladies in numerous nations. Likewise, contemporary developments have affected official changes connected with inappropriate behavior, regenerative privileges, and orientation based brutality.

Grassroots support fills in as a main impetus behind the push for legitimate changes, guaranteeing that the voices and worries of ladies are reflected in the regulations that oversee their lives.

Social Movements and Mindfulness:

Grassroots developments assume a significant part in molding social standards and testing well established generalizations. By bringing issues to light, starting troublesome discussions, and destroying restrictions, these developments add to a more extensive social shift toward orientation fairness. The #MeToo development, for example, has constrained social orders to go up against issues of working environment provocation and power uneven characters.

Grassroots drives not just feature the predominance of orientation based separation yet additionally encourage an aggregate retribution with cultural perspectives that propagate disparity.

Strengthening of Minimized People group:

Grassroots developments frequently center around the strengthening of minimized networks inside the more extensive battle for ladies' privileges. By tending to the extraordinary difficulties looked by ladies of variety, LGBTQ+ ladies, and those from financially hindered foundations, these developments take a stab at a more comprehensive and impartial type of strengthening.

Engaging underestimated networks isn't just a method for correcting verifiable treacheries yet in addition an essential way to deal with building a development that mirrors the variety of ladies' encounters.

Effect on Open Strategy:

The effect of grassroots developments reaches out to the domain of public arrangement, where backing endeavors impact the definition and execution of orientation delicate approaches. From work environment strategies addressing lewd behavior to medical care approaches perceiving regenerative freedoms, grassroots developments act as impetuses for molding strategy plans that focus on ladies' necessities.

The support model of grassroots developments, established in the lived encounters of ladies, adds to the improvement of additional responsive and successful strategies.

Extension of Multifaceted Women's liberation:

Grassroots developments play had a vital impact in extending the extent of woman's rights to embrace multifacetedness. By recognizing the interconnected idea of different types of separation, these developments guarantee that the battle for ladies' privileges is comprehensive and receptive to the assorted encounters, everything being equal.

Multifaceted woman's rights, as supported by grassroots drives, perceives that orientation uniformity can't be accomplished without tending to converging variables like race, class, and sexuality.

Difficulties and Future Contemplations:

While grassroots developments for ladies' privileges have accomplished huge triumphs, they additionally face difficulties that warrant consideration for supported progress.

Inclusivity and Interconnection:

Keeping up with inclusivity and interconnection inside grassroots developments requires constant exertion. Guaranteeing that the voices of underestimated networks are heard as well as effectively remembered for dynamic cycles is fundamental for making a development that mirrors the variety of ladies' encounters.

Manageability and Assets:

Grassroots developments frequently work with restricted assets, depending on the energy and devotion of activists. Supporting force over the long haul requires sufficient assets, hierarchical help, and key preparation. The test lies in adjusting the grassroots, local area driven nature of these developments with the requirement for supported influence.

Tending to Backfire and Opposition:

Grassroots developments can confront backfire and opposition from settled in power designs and those went against to cultural change. Beating obstruction requires strength, vital correspondence, and partnerships with steady partners. Building spans with people and gatherings outside the prompt development can assist with collecting more extensive help.

Worldwide Fortitude and Systems administration:

In an undeniably interconnected world, grassroots developments can profit from worldwide fortitude and systems administration. Sharing techniques, assets, and experiences across lines can intensify the effect of these developments and add to a more bound together front for ladies' privileges.

3.2 Activists and organizations leading the charge

The journey for ladies' freedoms and orientation balance has been progressed by a huge number of devoted activists and associations, whose indefatigable endeavors have become impetuses for social change. From grassroots developments to worldwide support organizations, these bosses play played critical parts in testing prejudicial works on, impacting strategy changes, and cultivating a more comprehensive world. This investigation digs into the narratives and effect of key activists and associations at the very front of the battle for ladies' privileges.

Individual Activists:

Malala Yousafzai:

Malala Yousafzai, Pakistani training dissident, rose to worldwide unmistakable quality for her valiant support for young ladies' schooling notwithstanding misfortune. Brought into the world in the Smack Valley, she challenged the Taliban's prohibition on young ladies going to class, prompting a designated assault on her in 2012. Malala endure the assault as well as strengthened her obligation to schooling, co-writing the journal "I'm Malala" and turning into the most youthful ever Nobel Prize laureate in 2014 at 17 years old. Through the Malala Asset, she keeps on supporting training as an essential ideal for each kid.

Tarana Burke:

Tarana Burke, an American social liberties dissident, is the organizer behind the #MeToo development. At first made to engage overcomers of sexual savagery, the development built up some decent forward movement as an energizing cry against lewd behavior and attack. Burke's work centers around the interconnection of the encounters looked by survivors, underscoring the significance of understanding the remarkable difficulties that various people and networks explore. Her grassroots activism has reshaped the talk on sexual brutality and incited a worldwide retribution with dug in power elements.

Emma Watson:

Emma Watson, an English entertainer and UN Ladies Generosity Diplomat, has turned into a vocal supporter for orientation correspondence. Through her HeForShe crusade, Watson urges men and young men to remain as partners in the battle for ladies' freedoms. Her ardent addresses at the Assembled Countries and commitment with worldwide pioneers have added to bringing issues to light about the significance of destroying orientation generalizations and encouraging inclusivity. Watson's backing stretches out past the screen, making her a conspicuous voice in the contemporary women's activist development.

Gloria Steinem:

Gloria Steinem, a spearheading American women's activist, writer, and social-political extremist, has been a main figure in the women's activist development since the 1960s. Fellow benefactor of Ms. magazine, Steinem has devoted her life to pushing for conceptive freedoms, orientation fairness, and civil rights. Her impact broadens universally, and her works, including the powerful article "In the event that Men Could Bleed," have tested winning standards and motivated ages of activists.

Associations at the Front:

UN Ladies:

UN Ladies, the Unified Countries element devoted to orientation balance and ladies' strengthening, assumes a focal part in planning worldwide endeavors to address orientation based separation. Through missions, for example, "HeForShe" and drives advancing ladies' monetary strengthening and political investment, UN Ladies attempts to propel orientation fairness on a worldwide scale. The association gives a stage to coordinated effort among states, common society, and people focused on understanding an existence where orientation balance is a reality.

Ladies' Walk Worldwide:

The Ladies' Walk, beginning in the US because of the 2016 official political decision, immediately developed into a worldwide development. Ladies' Walk Worldwide arranges and intensifies the endeavors of different grassroots associations and activists around the world. Through yearly walks, promotion missions, and local area commitment, the association advocates for ladies' freedoms, civil rights, and inclusivity. The decentralized idea of the Ladies' Walk takes into consideration different voices to add to an aggregate call for equity.

Plan Worldwide:

Plan Worldwide is a worldwide non-benefit association that spotlights on propelling kids' freedoms and balance for young ladies. With a presence in various nations, Plan Worldwide attempts to address the particular difficulties looked by young ladies, including admittance to training, medical services, and security from savagery. The association's drives expect to enable young ladies to declare their freedoms and add to building a more impartial world.

Balance Now:

Balance Presently is a global common freedoms association devoted to advancing and safeguarding the privileges of ladies and young ladies. Through legitimate support, missions, and organizations, Balance Currently resolves issues, for example, orientation based brutality, oppressive regulations, and destructive practices. The association attempts to consider state run administrations responsible for maintaining ladies' freedoms and looks for lawful change to internationally wipe out biased rehearses.

Significant Missions and Drives:

#HeForShe:

Sent off by UN Ladies and advocated by Emma Watson, the #HeForShe lobby approaches men and young men to help orientation equity effectively. The mission underlines that accomplishing orientation uniformity isn't exclusively a ladies' issue yet requires the aggregate endeavors of people, everything being equal. Through connecting with men as partners, #HeForShe looks to separate customary orientation standards and cultivate a more comprehensive comprehension of fairness.

#TimesUp:

Brought into the world in light of the #MeToo development, #TimesUp is a worldwide drive zeroed in on battling lewd behavior and orientation based segregation in work environments. The mission advocates for lawful changes, approaches that focus on work environment security, and social movements to guarantee responsibility for culprits. Time's Up underscores the significance of establishing conditions where people can work liberated from badgering and segregation.

Young ladies Not Ladies:

Young ladies Not Ladies is a worldwide organization focused on finishing kid marriage and empowering young ladies to live up to their true capacity. With individuals across the world, the association attempts to bring issues to light about the effect of kid marriage, advocate for strategy changes, and backing networks in forestalling this unsafe practice. Through aggregate activity, Young ladies Not Ladies tries to engage young ladies and make an existence where each kid can partake in their freedoms.

#BringBackOurGirls:

The #BringBackOurGirls lobby arose because of the capturing of school children by the fanatic gathering Boko Haram in Nigeria in 2014. Advocates, including Malala Yousafzai, called for global consideration and activity to protect the hijacked young ladies and address the more extensive issue of young ladies' admittance to schooling in struggle zones. While challenges continue, the mission carried worldwide attention to the situation of kidnapped young ladies and the more extensive issue of guaranteeing protected and available instruction for all.

Challenges and Diligent Issues:

Brutality Against Ladies:

Brutality against ladies stays an unavoidable worldwide issue, appearing in different structures like aggressive behavior at home, rape, and illegal exploitation. Activists and associations keep on standing up to the difficulties of tending to and forestalling viciousness, pushing for legitimate changes, and offering help for survivors. The MeToo and Time's Up developments have highlighted the commonness of provocation and attack, inciting calls for fundamental change.

Admittance to Instruction:

In spite of progress, boundaries to training persevere for some young ladies around the world. Unfair practices, social standards, and struggle related difficulties add to restricted admittance to quality instruction for young ladies. Advocates work to destroy these boundaries, advancing arrangements that guarantee equivalent instructive open doors for all kids, paying little heed to orientation.

Orientation Pay Hole:

The orientation pay hole stays a tenacious issue, with ladies procuring not exactly their male partners for a similar work. Backing endeavors center around advancing compensation straightforwardness, testing oppressive practices, and pushing for strategy changes to close the hole. Associations like the World Financial Discussion's Worldwide Orientation Hole Report feature abberations in monetary open doors and promoter for orientation comprehensive monetary approaches.

Conceptive Freedoms and Medical care:

Conceptive freedoms and medical care keep on being disagreeable issues, with discusses encompassing admittance to contraception, early termination, and far reaching regenerative medical care. Activists and associations work to guarantee that ladies have the independence to settle on conclusions about their bodies, admittance to conceptive medical care, and security from hurtful practices. This incorporates testing prohibitive regulations and upholding for approaches that focus on ladies' conceptive freedoms.

The Way Forward:

Multifaceted Promotion:

Perceiving and addressing the meeting factors that add to separation is fundamental for compelling promotion. Interconnected approaches guarantee that the privileges and encounters of ladies from different foundations are thought of, cultivating a more comprehensive and impartial development.

Worldwide Joint effort:

The battle for ladies' freedoms requires worldwide coordinated effort, with activists and associations working across lines to share systems, assets, and experiences. Building unions improves the aggregate effect of the development and reinforces the push for foundational change.

Lawful Changes and Responsibility:

Support endeavors should keep on zeroing in on legitimate changes that secure and maintain ladies' privileges. Considering state run administrations and organizations responsible for carrying out and upholding orientation touchy arrangements is vital for making enduring change.

Training and Mindfulness:

Training and mindfulness crusades stay imperative devices for testing generalizations, destroying hurtful standards, and encouraging a more orientation comprehensive society. Engaging people with information adds to a social shift that upholds balance.

Youth Commitment:

Including the more youthful age in support endeavors is basic for supporting energy and guaranteeing the proceeded with development of the ladies' freedoms development. Youth-drove drives, missions, and activism assume an essential part in molding the fate of orientation fairness.

3.3 Challenges faced in pushing for legislation

Supporting for regulation to advance orientation equity and ladies' freedoms is a diverse undertaking full of difficulties. While steps have been made internationally, the excursion toward thorough legitimate structures that address orientation differences is set apart by intricacies emerging from well established cultural standards, political obstruction, and foundational hindrances. This investigation digs into the horde challenges looked by activists, associations, and policymakers in the constant quest for regulation that maintains the standards of orientation correspondence.

1. **Well established Social and Cultural Standards:**

   One of the essential difficulties in pushing for orientation fairness regulation lies in profoundly settled in social and cultural standards. Conventional orientation jobs, generalizations, and assumptions frequently block progress, as they sustain oppressive practices and cutoff the extent of lawful changes. Conquering these instilled standards requires a nuanced approach that includes testing cultural mentalities through training, mindfulness missions, and encouraging comprehensive exchange.

2. **Political Opposition and Backfire:**

   The political scene can be an imposing hindrance to the institution of orientation fairness regulation. Obstruction from moderate groups, hesitance to challenge existing power structures, and the apprehension about reaction from constituents can slow down or sabotage regulative drives. Policymakers might be reluctant to support disputable measures, prompting a propagation of the state of affairs and a hesitance to challenge profoundly imbued orientation standards.

3. **Deficient Portrayal in Dynamic Bodies:**

   The absence of satisfactory portrayal of ladies in dynamic bodies represents a critical obstacle to the section of orientation correspondence regulation. At the point when regulative bodies are prevalently made out of men, there is a gamble that issues influencing ladies may not get the consideration and need they merit. Accomplishing orientation equality in political portrayal is a basic move toward guaranteeing that regulative plans are intelligent of different viewpoints and receptive to the requirements, all things considered.

4. **Conflicting Legitimate Structures:**

   In numerous purviews, existing lawful systems might be conflicting or lacking to address the intricacies of orientation based separation extensively. Holes in regulation, disconnected arrangements, and the shortfall of explicit assurances for minimized bunches add to a climate where equity is tricky. Advocates should explore these irregularities and work toward making complete, enforceable lawful structures that rule out uncertainty.

5. **Absence of Execution and Requirement Systems:**

   In any event, when moderate orientation balance regulation is established, the absence of hearty execution and requirement systems represents a significant test. Deficient assets, inadequate preparation of policing, and an absence of responsibility measures can subvert the expected effect of regulation. Overcoming any barrier between legitimate structures and powerful execution is critical for guaranteeing that the privileges revered in regulation are substantial real factors for people.

6. **Monetary Disparities:**

   Monetary variations between sexual orientations add to the difficulties looked in pushing for orientation correspondence regulation. Ladies, especially those from underestimated networks, may miss the mark on monetary assets and freedom expected to successfully participate in backing endeavors. Monetary disparities can restrict admittance to legitimate portrayal, thwart cooperation in political cycles, and propagate a pattern of drawback that hinders progress toward orientation fairness.

7. **Resistance from Moderate Organizations:**

   Much of the time, moderate organizations, including strict substances and moderate instructive foundations, may go against moderate orientation balance regulation. Resistance from these quarters can apply significant effect on general assessment and influence political direction. Exploring this resistance requires talented discussion, taking part in valuable exchange, and building coalitions with assorted partners to connect philosophical holes.

8. **Absence of Diversity in Regulation:**

   Orientation imbalance meets with different types of segregation, like race, class, and sexual direction. Regulation that neglects to represent these converging personalities can coincidentally sustain abberations. Advocates face the test of guaranteeing that orientation balance regulation is interconnected, tending to the exceptional difficulties looked by people who have a place with various underestimated gatherings. This requires an extensive comprehension of the interconnected idea of separation and a guarantee to comprehensive strategy making.

9. **Public Discernments and Generalizations:**

   Public insights and generalizations about orientation jobs can altogether impact the outcome of authoritative endeavors. Misguided judgments about the objectives of orientation equity regulation, fears of seen dangers to conventional qualities, and protection from change can establish a difficult climate for support. Moving public insights requires key correspondence, training efforts, and narrating that refines the encounters of those affected by orientation imbalance.

10. **Worldwide Disparities and Varying Needs:**
    The worldwide idea of orientation disparity implies that difficulties looked in pushing for regulation can differ fundamentally across districts. In certain unique situations, quick worries like monetary turn of events, political steadiness, or struggle might outweigh orientation fairness drives. Connecting these worldwide imbalances and adjusting needs to perceive the direness of tending to orientation incongruities requires discretion, global coordinated effort, and a common obligation to basic freedoms.

11. **Lawful Difficulties and Sacred Boundaries:**
    Now and again, sacred boundaries might block the advancement of orientation fairness regulation. Legitimate systems that unequivocally or verifiably separate in view of orientation can make huge obstacles. Advocates should explore sacred difficulties, now and again requiring established alterations or lawful understandings that line up with standards of balance and equity.

12. **Absence of Information and Exploration:**

A deficiency of thorough information and exploration on orientation inconsistencies can impede backing endeavors. Information holes make it trying to fabricate proof based contentions, evaluate the effect of unfair practices, and really convey the earnestness of administrative changes. Connecting these holes requires interest in research, information assortment, and the advancement of solid measurements to survey the viability of orientation balance regulation.

Chapter 4

The Controversy Surrounding Women's Reservation

The issue of ladies' booking in political circles has been a subject of extraordinary discussion and contention, mirroring the intricacies and disparate viewpoints inside society. The proposition to save a specific level of seats for ladies in regulative bodies means to address orientation variations in political portrayal, yet it has experienced obstruction and analysis on different fronts. This investigation dives into the complex contentions encompassing ladies' booking, looking at the contentions both for and against this governmental policy regarding minorities in society measure.

Contentions in Favor:

Tending to Orientation Abberations:

Defenders of ladies' booking contend that it is an essential and positive move toward address verifiable and foundational orientation differences in political portrayal.

Ladies have been generally underrepresented in official bodies, and reservations give a designated component to overcome this issue. By guaranteeing a base portrayal of ladies, reservations try to make a more comprehensive and various political scene.

Upgrading Ladies' Investment:

One of the essential objectives of ladies' booking is to upgrade the dynamic cooperation of ladies in dynamic cycles. Advocates battle that expanded portrayal is essential for enhancing ladies' voices on issues that straightforwardly influence them. Having ladies in regulative bodies is viewed as a way to bring different viewpoints, needs, and encounters to the very front, enhancing strategy conversations and adding to more comprehensive direction.

Breaking Male centric Standards:

Ladies' booking is seen as a device to challenge and separate male centric standards that have generally consigned ladies to optional jobs in political fields. By making space for ladies in dynamic jobs, reservations mean to challenge generalizations, disturb orientation standards, and advance the possibility that ladies can be powerful pioneers fit for molding public arrangement.

Job Demonstrating and Strengthening:

Expanded portrayal of ladies in legislative issues is viewed as an integral asset for job demonstrating and strengthening. At the point when ladies see different ladies involving places of political power, it can rouse desires and add to destroying boundaries to ladies' political support. Ladies in administrative roles become noticeable images of strengthening, empowering others to participate in political cycles.

Further developed Approach Results:

Advocates contend that different portrayal prompts more thorough strategy results. Ladies, they contend, frequently carry a remarkable viewpoint to administration, with an emphasis on issues like instruction, medical services, and social government assistance. Reservations, consequently, are seen as a way to make regulative bodies that better reflect and answer the requirements of the whole populace.

Contentions Against:

Meritocracy and Capability:

A vital conflict against ladies' booking spins around the standard of meritocracy. Rivals contend that political portrayal ought to be founded on individual legitimacy and skill as opposed to orientation. They state that reservations might think twice about determination of the top up-and-comers, possibly prompting a reduction in the general capability of regulative bodies.

Hypocrisy and Sabotaging Capability:

Pundits express worry that ladies' booking might prompt hypocrisy, where ladies chose through reservations are seen as emblematic placeholders instead of people picked for their capacities. This discernment, they contend, can subvert the validity and viability of ladies in political jobs, building up generalizations about ladies' skill.

Intra-Orientation Inconsistencies:

A few rivals feature the potential for intra-orientation inconsistencies, where ladies from special foundations may excessively profit from reservations, leaving minimized and hindered ladies underrepresented. Pundits stress the significance of addressing interconnection to guarantee that reservations benefit a different range of ladies.

Sacred and Legitimate Worries:

There are established and lawful worries raised against ladies' booking, basically connected with the standard of equity. Rivals contend that reservations in light of orientation might be viewed as biased and in spite of the standard of equivalent open door. The test lies in finding some kind of harmony between governmental policy regarding minorities in society and the sacred assurance of balance.

Potentially negative results:

Pundits express worries about unseen side-effects, for example, the potential for reservations to build up orientation generalizations or sustain existing power structures. There is a trepidation that the emphasis on reservations could divert from resolving further fundamental issues that add to orientation variations, like social standards and inconsistent admittance to schooling.

Political Obstruction:

Past these particular contentions, ladies' booking faces political obstruction that frequently reflects more extensive power elements and institutional difficulties:

Political Backfire:

Political protection from ladies' booking can appear as a type of reaction against saw dangers to existing power structures. Laid out political figures, especially men, may oppose the rearrangement of seats, dreading a weakening of their impact. This political opposition can be a huge obstacle in getting the vital official help for ladies' booking.

Party Elements:

Ideological groups might display inner elements that add to obstruction against ladies' booking. While certain gatherings effectively champion orientation fairness, others might focus on keeping up with existing power designs and oppose interior changes that challenge customary standards.

Absence of Agreement:

Accomplishing agreement among different ideological groups on the execution of ladies' booking can be a considerable test. Contrasts in philosophies, discretionary techniques, and local contemplations can block the development of a bound together front on the side of orientation equity measures.

Lacking Political Will:

The execution of ladies' booking requires political will and responsibility from pioneers at different levels. In situations where pioneers are reluctant to advocate orientation uniformity gauges, the absence of political will can hinder progress in spite of the squeezing need for regulative changes.

4.1 Opposition and criticisms

The proposition for ladies' booking in political circles, while planning to address orientation differences, has been met with vigorous resistance and reactions from different quarters. The resistance to this governmental policy regarding minorities in society measure is different, enveloping worries connected with its effect on meritocracy, the potential for hypocrisy, and more extensive philosophical and established contemplations. This investigation digs into the diverse resistance and reactions encompassing ladies' booking, taking apart the contentions against this strategy and revealing insight into the intricacies that underlie the talk.

1. **Meritocracy and Ability:**

   One of the essential reactions evened out against ladies' booking spins around the rule of meritocracy. Pundits contend that political portrayal ought to be founded on individual legitimacy, ability, and capabilities as opposed to orientation. The trepidation is that carrying out reservations might think twice about choice of the top up-and-comers, possibly prompting a decrease in the general skill of regulative bodies. This contention puts accentuation on the possibility that up-and-comers, paying little heed to orientation, ought to be chosen in view of their abilities and history as opposed to segment qualities.

2. **Hypocrisy and Subverting Capability:**
A huge concern related with ladies' booking is the potential for hypocrisy, where ladies chose through reservations might be seen as representative placeholders as opposed to people picked for their capacities. Pundits contend that this discernment can sabotage the validity and adequacy of ladies in political jobs, building up generalizations about ladies' skill. The trepidation is that reservations could coincidentally propagate the thought that ladies need exceptional measures to enter legislative issues, as opposed to being chosen in view of their abilities and achievements.

3. **Intra-Orientation Abberations:**
Pundits feature the potential for intra-orientation differences as a basic downside of ladies' booking.
There is a worry that ladies from favored foundations may excessively profit from reservations, leaving underestimated and impeded ladies underrepresented. The analysis underscores the significance of addressing interconnection to guarantee that reservations benefit a different range of ladies, representing elements, for example, financial status, standing, and geographic area.

4. **Sacred and Legitimate Worries:**
Rivals of ladies' booking raise sacred and legitimate worries, principally connected with the rule of balance. Pundits contend that reservations in view of orientation might be seen as unfair and in spite of the protected assurance of equivalent open door. Finding some kind of harmony between governmental policy regarding minorities in society and guaranteeing equivalent open doors for all residents turns into a sensitive undertaking, requiring cautious thought of protected standards.

5. **Potentially negative results:**
There are worries about potentially negative results related with ladies' booking. Pundits stress that the emphasis on reservations could divert from resolving further fundamental issues that add to orientation incongruities, like social standards and inconsistent admittance to instruction. There is a trepidation that the accentuation on standards might eclipse the requirement for extensive cultural and institutional changes to advance orientation equity.

6. **Political Kickback:**
Political obstruction and reaction against ladies' booking manifest as resistance from laid out political figures, especially men, who might oppose the rearrangement of seats, dreading a weakening of their impact. This type of obstruction mirrors the more extensive test of reshaping power structures inside political circles. Occupant government officials might oppose changes that might actually modify business as usual and challenge conventional standards.

7. **Party Elements:**
Interior elements inside ideological groups add to resistance against ladies' booking. While certain gatherings effectively champion orientation uniformity,

others might focus on keeping up with existing power designs and oppose inner changes that challenge conventional standards. Philosophical contrasts, constituent methodologies, and local contemplations can prevent the development of a bound together front on the side of orientation fairness measures.

8. **Absence of Agreement:**
Accomplishing agreement among different ideological groups on the execution of ladies' booking can be an imposing test. Contrasts in philosophies, constituent methodologies, and provincial contemplations can block the development of a brought together front on the side of orientation correspondence measures. Absence of agreement represents a critical snag to the regulative cycle, as differing needs and political estimations become an integral factor.

9. **Lacking Political Will:**
The fruitful execution of ladies' booking requires political will and responsibility from pioneers at different levels. In situations where pioneers are reluctant to advocate orientation uniformity gauges, the absence of political will can block progress notwithstanding the squeezing need for administrative changes. Conquering this challenge requires an aggregate obligation to propelling orientation equity inside political circles.

10. **Likely Effect on Discretionary Elements:**

Pundits express worries about the expected effect of ladies' booking on constituent elements. A contend that reservations might prompt the essential situation of ladies competitors exclusively to meet the ordered shares, possibly changing the elements of political rivalry. The trepidation is that this could bring about strategic selections instead of a veritable obligation to propelling ladies' political investment.

1. **Misconceptions and myths**

The talk encompassing ladies' booking in political circles is frequently obfuscated by misinterpretations and fantasies that add to opposition and wariness. These misinterpretations, established in social, social, and political accounts, shape popular assessment and impact strategy discusses. Disentangling these legends is fundamental for a nuanced comprehension of the intricacies related with governmental policy regarding minorities in society measures. This investigation digs into normal misinterpretations and fantasies encompassing ladies' booking, revealing insight into the real factors that underlie the talk.

1. **Fantasy: Ladies' Booking Is an Attack against Meritocracy:**
One predominant fantasy encompassing ladies' booking is that it sabotages meritocracy by focusing on orientation over capabilities. Pundits contend that political portrayal ought to be founded exclusively on legitimacy and capability

as opposed to segment attributes. Nonetheless, advocates fight that ladies' booking isn't tied in with forfeiting merit however tending to verifiable and fundamental predispositions that have brought about the underrepresentation of ladies. Reservations mean to set out equivalent open doors for qualified ladies to partake in political cycles, guaranteeing that legitimacy is viewed as inside a more comprehensive system.

2. **Legend: Reservations Lead to Hypocrisy and Ineffectual Initiative:**
There is a boundless misguided judgment that ladies chose through reservations may be seen as simple tokens, involving positions emblematically instead of contributing successfully. Pundits express worries that this apparent posturing could subvert the believability and adequacy of ladies in political jobs. In any case, examination and true models counter this fantasy, showing that ladies chose through reservations have frequently areas of strength for exhibited characteristics, successfully addressing their bodies electorate, and contributing definitively to strategy conversations.

3. **Legend: Ladies' Booking Is a Panacea for Orientation Disparity:**
While ladies' booking is an essential move toward tending to orientation incongruities, there is a misinterpretation that it alone can kill all types of orientation imbalance. Truly, reservations are essential for a more extensive methodology that incorporates social movements, instructive changes, and institutional changes. Ladies' booking plans to make an underlying pathway for ladies' political investment however doesn't refute the requirement for far reaching cultural change to accomplish orientation equity.

4. **Fantasy: Ladies Need Interest or Ability in Legislative issues:**
A tenacious legend is the presumption that ladies need interest or skill in governmental issues, legitimizing their underrepresentation. This conviction supports orientation generalizations and neglects foundational boundaries that limit ladies' entrance into political fields. Research shows that whenever offered the chance, ladies are similarly skilled and keen on political authority. Ladies' booking tries to challenge this legend by establishing a climate that energizes and upholds ladies' dynamic cooperation in governmental issues.

5. **Legend: Reservations Disregard Financial and Social Variety:**
Some contend that ladies' booking misrepresents the intricacies of variety by zeroing in exclusively on orientation. Pundits express worries about ignoring financial and social factors that add to imbalances among ladies. As a general rule, defenders of reservations perceive the requirement for a multifaceted methodology, recognizing the different encounters of ladies in view of elements like standing, class, and geographic area. Endeavors are made to guarantee that ladies from all foundations benefit from governmental policy regarding minorities in society measures.

6. **Fantasy: Reservations Are a Burden on Equitable Cycles:**
There is a misinterpretation that ladies' booking is a burden on just cycles,

encroaching upon the standards of free and fair decisions. Rivals contend that up-and-comers ought to be chosen in view of famous help as opposed to fore-ordained portions. Defenders counter this by stressing that reservations are a restorative measure to address verifiable predispositions, guaranteeing that majority rule processes become more comprehensive and intelligent of the different populace.

7. **Legend: Ladies' Booking Is a Transitory Fix:**
Another misinterpretation is that ladies' booking is a transitory fix that will lose pertinence once orientation inconsistencies are tended to. Truly, reservations are seen as an impetus for long haul change, cultivating a world of politics where ladies can logically contend on neutral ground. The point is to make a level battleground that will persevere until fundamental hindrances to ladies' political support are destroyed.

8. **Legend: Reservations Lead to Family Intermediary Rule:**
Pundits frequently contend that ladies chose through reservations could become intermediaries for male relatives, propagating dynastic governmental issues. While occurrences of family impact exist in governmental issues, research proposes that ladies chose through reservations have exhibited free direction and authority. Reservations mean to break the hindrances that ruin ladies from entering governmental issues independently, testing the fantasy of ladies as simple expansions of male relatives.

9. **Legend: Ladies' Booking Is About Numbers, As opposed to Effect:**
Some see ladies' booking as a simple numbers game disregarding its more extensive effect. Pundits contend that rising the quantity of ladies in political positions doesn't be guaranteed to prompt significant strategy changes. Defenders counter this fantasy by featuring the groundbreaking capability of expanded portrayal. Research demonstrates that assorted lawmaking bodies lead to more exhaustive arrangement results, testing the thought that mathematical portrayal alone is immaterial.

10. **Fantasy: Reservations Are a Danger to Conventional Qualities:**

Rivals of ladies' booking might contend that it represents a danger to conventional qualities or disturbs laid out power structures. This legend reflects worries about cultural standards and protection from change. Advocates pressure that ladies' booking lines up with popularity based upsides of inclusivity and equivalent portrayal, enhancing political talk without intrinsically testing customary qualities.

b. Political and cultural resistance

The excursion towards executing ladies' booking in political circles has been set apart by a mind boggling exchange of political and social obstruction. Notwithstanding the undeniable cases for governmental policy regarding minorities in society measures to address orientation differences, resistance from different quarters has presented imposing difficulties. This investigation digs into the elements of political and social obstruction, unwinding the intricacies that thwart the full acknowledgment of ladies' booking.

Political Opposition:

Danger to Existing Power Designs:

One of the essential purposes behind political protection from ladies' booking lies in the apparent danger to existing power structures. Political scenes, particularly those generally overwhelmed by men, frequently oppose rearranging seats to oblige ladies. Occupant legislators might see expanded portrayal for ladies as a weakening of their impact, prompting opposition against strategy changes that challenge conventional standards.

Feeling of dread toward Discretionary Kickback:

Political pioneers, especially in popular governments, may fear appointive reaction from constituents who might oppose changes to business as usual. Upholding for ladies' booking should be visible as a possibly disagreeable move, especially in social orders where well established orientation standards persevere. The apprehension about losing votes or confronting resistance from moderate groups can frustrate political will to support orientation balance measures.

Party Elements and Inside Resistance:

Inside ideological groups, inward elements can add to obstruction against ladies' booking. A few gatherings might oppose interior changes that challenge conventional standards, and philosophical contrasts among party individuals might prompt inward resistance. Accomplishing an agreement inside ideological groups on the execution of ladies' booking can be a huge obstacle, as clashing needs and vital contemplations become possibly the most important factor.

Absence of Prioritization:

At times, political pioneers may not focus on orientation equity or ladies' issues because of a discernment that other squeezing matters, for example, monetary turn of events or security concerns, outweigh everything else. The absence of prioritization can bring about a hesitance to distribute assets, time, and political money to propel strategies pointed toward expanding ladies' portrayal in legislative issues.

Deficient Portrayal of Ladies in Dynamic Bodies:

The absence of satisfactory portrayal of ladies in dynamic bodies adds to political obstruction against ladies' booking. At the point when regulative bodies are prevalently made out of men, there might be an absence of compassion and understanding in regards to the desperation and significance of tending to orientation variations. Accomplishing orientation equality in political portrayal is a critical stage in beating this obstruction.

Social Obstruction:

Well established Orientation Standards and Generalizations:

Social protection from ladies' booking is well established in cultural orientation standards and generalizations. Conventional assumptions about the jobs of people in the public eye frequently impact popular assessment and protection from changes in power elements. Generalizations that question ladies' skill in political administration can propagate social protection from expanded portrayal for ladies.

Obstruction from Moderate Foundations:

Moderate organizations, including strict elements and moderate instructive foundations, may effectively oppose moderate orientation correspondence estimates like ladies' booking. Resistance from these quarters can be a critical obstruction, as they frequently employ impact over general assessment and may shape political stories that add to social opposition against strategies testing conventional orientation jobs.

Cultural Impression of Ladies in Authority:

Cultural impression of ladies in positions of authority assume a urgent part in molding social obstruction. Firmly established convictions about the suitable jobs for ladies might bring about doubt about their capacity to lead really in political circles. Changing these discernments requires a complex methodology that difficulties generalizations, features effective ladies pioneers, and cultivates a more comprehensive comprehension of initiative.

Anxiety toward Disturbing Social Congruity:

Social obstruction may likewise come from a feeling of dread toward disturbing social concordance or existing local area structures. In social orders where orientation jobs are profoundly imbued, the possibility of ladies expecting more conspicuous jobs in legislative issues might be met with opposition because of worries about disturbing laid out friendly orders. Crossing over this social obstruction requires nuanced approaches that address fears and feature the advantages of orientation equity.

Authentic Inheritances and Social Dormancy:

Authentic traditions of man controlled society and social dormancy add to opposition against ladies' booking. In social orders where power elements have been customarily male-overwhelmed, social standards and practices might be profoundly dug in. Conquering this opposition requires a drawn out obligation to social change, testing instilled convictions, and cultivating new stories that embrace orientation equity.

Defeating Opposition:

Key Promotion and Correspondence:

Key support and correspondence are fundamental for conquering both political and social obstruction. Outlining the conversation in a manner that stresses the advantages of ladies' cooperation in governmental issues, the significance of different viewpoints, and the positive effect on administration can assist with moving general assessment and collect political help.

Building Unions and Alliances:

Building partnerships and alliances with different partners, including common society associations, ladies' gatherings, and moderate components inside ideological groups, can make a unified front against obstruction. Cooperative endeavors enhance the effect of backing and give a more extensive base of help for ladies' booking.

Legitimate Changes and Institutional Changes:

Executing legitimate changes and institutional changes that help orientation correspondence is significant for conquering opposition. Guaranteeing that regulations are set up to safeguard ladies' freedoms, advance equivalent open doors, and implement orientation delicate strategies makes an establishment for destroying obstructions.

Instruction and Mindfulness Missions:

Training and mindfulness crusades assume a significant part in testing social obstruction. These missions can expose legends, feature examples of overcoming adversity of ladies pioneers, and cultivate a more comprehensive comprehension of orientation jobs. Instructive drives that advance orientation awareness since the beginning add to social change.

Worldwide Cooperation and Strain:

Worldwide cooperation and strain can be instrumental in conquering obstruction, particularly in situations where states might be reluctant to advocate orientation uniformity measures. Drawing in with worldwide bodies, sharing prescribed procedures, and utilizing worldwide organizations can make energy for change.

4.2 Debates within feminist circles

Inside the far reaching domain of women's activist talk, there exists a lively and dynamic embroidery of points of view, belief systems, and discussions. Women's activist circles are described by a variety of thought, mirroring the perplexing crossing points of character, culture, and socio-political settings. This investigation digs into a portion of the vital discussions inside women's activist circles, featuring the nuanced conversations that shape the development.

1. **Multifacetedness:**

   At the core of contemporary women's activist discussions is the idea of multifacetedness, presented by Kimberlé Crenshaw. This system underlines the interconnected idea of social classes like orientation, race, class, and sexuality. While diversity has been generally embraced for its inclusivity, banters inside women's activist circles frequently spin around the affirmation and prioritization of different crossing personalities. Some contend for a more far reaching comprehension of multifacetedness, while others fight that specific perspectives, like race or class, may be eclipsed inside the more extensive talk.

2. **Liberal Woman's rights versus Revolutionary Women's liberation:**

   The continuous discussion between liberal woman's rights and extremist women's liberation reflects different ways to deal with accomplishing orientation correspondence. Liberal women's activists advocate for steady changes inside existing designs, accentuating legitimate changes and equivalent open doors.

   Then again, extremist women's activists investigate the actual groundworks of male centric designs and call for extraordinary, progressive change. The discussion between these two points of view rotates around inquiries of system, the speed of progress, and the degree to which cultural designs should be destroyed or improved.

3. **Sex-Positive versus Sex-Negative Women's liberation:**
   One more noticeable discussion focuses on perspectives towards sexuality inside women's activist circles. Sex-positive women's activists embrace a confirming perspective on sexuality, underlining sexual organization, freedom, and the destroying of sexual restrictions. On the other hand, sex-negative women's activists express worries about the typification of ladies, the effect of porn, and the propagation of hurtful sexual standards. The pressure between these viewpoints highlights the perplexing relationship women's activists have with sexuality and the difficulties of exploring a different scope of perspectives towards it.

4. **Worldwide Woman's rights and Social Relativism:**
   The globalization of women's activist talk has prompted banters around social relativism and the use of Western women's activist structures to different worldwide settings. Some contend for a more nuanced figuring out that regards social contrasts and integrates neighborhood points of view. Others keep up with that specific widespread standards, like common freedoms and orientation fairness, ought to outweigh everything else. The strain lies in tracking down a harmony between recognizing social variety and upholding for basic freedoms without forcing ethnocentric qualities.

5. **Trans-Comprehensive Women s liberation:**
   The incorporation of transsexual people inside women's activist spaces has arisen as a petulant issue. While numerous women's activists advocate for a diverse and trans-comprehensive methodology, others express worries about the ramifications for the encounters of cisgender ladies. Discusses center around the meaning of womanhood, the convergence of orientation and science, and the consideration of transsexual points of view in conversations around regenerative freedoms, brutality against ladies, and other key women's activist issues.

6. **Decision Women's liberation versus Primary Change:**
   The strain between individual decisions and primary change is a repetitive subject inside women's activist discussions. Decision women's liberation stresses individual independence and the option to settle on private decisions without judgment. Pundits contend that this point of view can neglect foundational obstructions and build up existing disparities. The discussion fixates on whether zeroing in on individual office is adequate for accomplishing orientation balance or on the other hand in the event that more extensive underlying changes are basic to address foundational treacheries.

7. **Corporate Women's liberation and Neoliberalism:**
   The hug of women's activist topics by partnerships and the mainstreaming of woman's rights have started banters about co-optation and the commodifica-tion of women's activist goals. Some contend that corporate women's liberation adds to the weakening of extremist objectives, transforming woman's rights into an attractive brand. Others consider it to be a technique to bring women's activist issues into standard cognizance. The discussion highlights inquiries of

credibility, corporate responsibility, and the potential for significant change inside existing entrepreneur structures.

8. **Parenthood and Regenerative Privileges:**
Women's activist circles wrestle with assorted points of view on parenthood and conceptive privileges. While certain women's activists underline the option to pick the decision about whether to become moms, others scrutinize cultural assumptions around parenthood and the difficulties looked by the people who decide to focus on their vocations. The discussion likewise stretches out to conversations about the commodification of regenerative innovations and the ramifications for minimized networks.

9. **Computerized Woman's rights and Online Activism:**
The approach of computerized woman's rights and online activism has acquainted new aspects with women's activist discussions. Conversations rotate around the adequacy of online stages in cultivating comprehensive discourse, the potential for online spaces to become protected, closed off areas, and the convergence among computerized and disconnected activism. Banters inside women's activist circles question the democratizing capability of advanced spaces while likewise recognizing the difficulties of exploring on the web provocation and poisonousness.

10. **Ecofeminism and Natural Equity:**

The crossing point of woman's rights and environmentalism has led to ecofeminism, a viewpoint that investigates the associations between the double-dealing of ladies and the double-dealing of the climate. Banters inside this system spin around the prioritization of natural issues inside women's activist talk, the effect of environmental change on ladies, and the job of ecofeminism in more extensive civil rights developments.

1. Intersectionality and inclusivity

In the steadily developing scene of civil rights and activism, the idea of multifacetedness has arisen as a strong structure that tries to comprehend and address the interconnected idea of social classifications like race, orientation, class, sexuality, from there, the sky is the limit. Begat by Kimberlé Crenshaw in the last part of the 1980s, multifacetedness has turned into a foundation of contemporary women's activist talk, stressing the need to perceive the mind boggling manners by which different parts of personality cross and shape people's encounters.

1. **Characterizing Diversity:**
At its center, diversity challenges oversimplified and one-layered understandings of character. It recognizes that people exist at the convergences of various social

classifications, and these crossing points make remarkable and frequently complex encounters. For instance, an Individual of color's experience isn't exclusively molded by her race or orientation freely however by the interchange of the two elements alongside different components of her character.

2. **The Interconnected Trap of Characters:**
   The figurative trap of meeting personalities represents how different viewpoints like race, orientation, class, sexuality, handicap, and more are interconnected. These convergences make a variety of points of view and encounters that can't be completely perceived by looking at individual personality markers in detachment. Perceiving this interconnectedness is fundamental to building a more comprehensive and nuanced comprehension of social issues.

3. **Inclusivity Past Single-Issue Promotion:**
   Multifacetedness requires a shift from single-issue backing to a more exhaustive and comprehensive methodology. It urges activists and supporters to consider the more extensive setting where social issues unfurl. For example, tending to orientation imbalance requires an assessment of how race, class, and different elements converge with orientation, impacting the encounters of various gatherings of ladies in assorted ways.

4. **Recognizing Honor and Abuse:**
   A vital part of diversity is the acknowledgment of honor and persecution. People might encounter honor in specific parts of their personality while confronting mistreatment in others. For instance, a cisgender hetero lady might encounter orientation based separation yet holds honor concerning cisnormativity and heteronormativity. Understanding and recognizing these elements are fundamental for building fortitude and cultivating allyship.

5. **Difficulties to a Homogeneous Women's liberation:**
   Diversity challenges the thought of a homogeneous women's liberation that tends to the worries of a tight segment. It stands up against a one-size-fits-all methodology and urges women's activists to think about the different necessities and encounters of ladies from different foundations. In doing as such, multifacetedness maintains a strategic distance from the eradication of underestimated voices inside women's activist developments.

6. **Strategy Suggestions:**
   The multifaceted focal point has critical ramifications for strategy making. Strategies that neglect to represent the convergences of character may incidentally sustain imbalances. For instance, orientation based arrangements that don't consider racial or financial elements may lopsidedly help specific gatherings of ladies while leaving others minimized. Multifaceted arrangement examination is fundamental for making complete and powerful arrangements.

7. **Challenges in Execution:**
   While multifacetedness offers a strong hypothetical structure, its execution faces difficulties. The intricacy of meeting characters makes it challenging to foster

one-size-fits-all arrangements. The pragmatic use of multifacetedness requires progressing discourse, adaptability, and a guarantee to figuring out the remarkable encounters of people inside unambiguous settings.

8. **Comprehensive Language and Portrayal:**
The significance of utilizing comprehensive language and guaranteeing different portrayal couldn't possibly be more significant in that frame of mind of diversity. Language shapes how we might interpret social issues, and portrayal matters in approving different encounters. Endeavors to utilize language that recognizes and regards the complexities of personality add to making more comprehensive spaces.

9. **Instruction and Mindfulness:**
Training and mindfulness assume a urgent part in advancing multifacetedness. Consolidating interconnected points of view into instructive educational programs encourages a comprehension of different encounters and difficulties cliché stories. Furthermore, mindfulness crusades that feature the accounts of people at the crossing points of different characters add to destroying inclinations and cultivating sympathy.

10. **Transnational Multifacetedness:**

Multifacetedness reaches out past public boundaries, accentuating the significance of thinking about worldwide points of view. Transnational multifacetedness perceives that issues like movement, globalization, and pilgrim heritages cross with social classes, impacting people's encounters on a worldwide scale. Promotion for civil rights, consequently, requires a comprehension of the interconnectedness of issues across various international settings.

Chapter 5

Legislative Progress and Setbacks

The excursion toward accomplishing orientation uniformity through authoritative measures has been portrayed by both outstanding advancement and critical misfortunes. Across the globe, official drives have tried to address authentic imbalances, advance ladies' privileges, and destroy foundational boundaries. Notwithstanding, the way toward meaningful and getting through change is loaded with intricacies, mirroring the multi-layered difficulties that persevere in different social orders. This investigation dives into the official headway made in propelling orientation fairness and the constant difficulties that highlight the continuous battle for an additional comprehensive and impartial world.

1. **Milestone Accomplishments:**
   Throughout the long term, regulative achievements play had a critical impact in propelling orientation equity. Testimonial developments in the mid twentieth century tied down ladies' more right than wrong to cast a ballot in a few nations, denoting a groundbreaking change in political support. The foundation of lawful systems precluding segregation based on orientation in schooling, work, and public administrations has been a huge step in the right direction. Also, regulation tending to aggressive behavior at home, inappropriate behavior, and conceptive freedoms has tried to safeguard ladies' independence and prosperity.

2. **Share Frameworks and Governmental policy regarding minorities in society:**
   Numerous nations have executed share frameworks and governmental policy regarding minorities in society measures to address the underrepresentation of ladies in political, monetary, and instructive circles. Portions for ladies in political authority, for example, official seats or bureau positions, mean to break settled in orientation standards and increment ladies' perceivability and impact in dynamic cycles. While these actions have added to eminent additions in certain districts, they likewise face opposition and analysis.

3. **Maternity and Paternity Leave Arrangements:**
Official drives around maternity and paternity leave ponder advancing viewpoints orientation jobs and balance between serious and fun activities. Strategies that give paid pass on to new moms and fathers add to a more impartial dissemination of providing care liabilities. Notwithstanding, challenges continue guaranteeing the execution and requirement of such arrangements, and abberations in admittance to parental leave can sustain orientation based disparities in the labor force.

4. **Equivalent Compensation Regulation:**
Endeavors to address the orientation pay hole through regulation have picked up speed. Different nations have instituted regulations advancing equivalent compensation for equivalent work, intending to wipe out wage abberations among people. Notwithstanding these official measures, accomplishing genuine compensation value stays a complicated test, impacted by variables like word related isolation, oblivious inclination, and cultural assumptions.

5. **Legitimate Assurances Against Savagery:**
Regulation pointed toward forestalling and tending to brutality against ladies has been a point of convergence chasing orientation balance. Regulations condemning aggressive behavior at home, rape, and illegal exploitation give a lawful structure to safeguard survivors and consider culprits responsible. Notwithstanding, the execution and requirement of these regulations face obstructions, including social standards that propagate casualty accusing and the belittling of survivors.

6. **Challenges in Execution:**
While regulative advancement is a urgent step, challenges in execution frequently thwart the acknowledgment of planned results. Insufficient implementation components, social opposition, and foundational inclinations inside legitimate establishments can obstruct the compelling execution of orientation equity regulations. Besides, abberations in admittance to legitimate assets and consciousness of freedoms add to lopsided results, especially for minimized networks.

7. **Backfire and Resistance:**
In spite of regulative steps, orientation fairness gauges regularly experience kickback and resistance.
Profoundly instilled man centric standards, social opposition, and moderate belief systems can subvert the execution of moderate regulations. At times, there is a hesitance to challenge conventional power structures, and regulative increases face the gamble of being moved back or weakened.

8. **Lawful Difficulties to Conceptive Freedoms:**
Regenerative freedoms, including admittance to contraception and safe fetus removal, have been disagreeable lawful landmarks. Administrative endeavors to confine or shorten conceptive privileges can lopsidedly influence ladies' independence and wellbeing. Legitimate difficulties, frequently determined by

philosophical and strict contemplations, feature the continuous battle to get and safeguard conceptive opportunities.

9. **Worldwide Points of view and Social Responsiveness:**
The worldwide idea of the journey for orientation equity requires a comprehension of assorted social settings. Regulation should explore the sensitive harmony between all inclusive basic freedoms standards and regarding social subtleties. Finding some kind of harmony requires nuanced approaches that recognize the organization of ladies inside their particular social, strict, and social settings.

10. **The Job of Grassroots Developments:**
Grassroots developments and activism play had a urgent impact in driving regulative change. Developments like #MeToo have uncovered the commonness of lewd behavior and attack, provoking regulative reactions and cultural movements. Grassroots preparation has the ability to impact general assessment, earn political will, and consider administrators responsible for focusing on orientation balance issues.

11. **Determined Holes and Incomplete Plans:**

In spite of authoritative progressions, tenacious holes in orientation balance remain, flagging incomplete plans. Issues, for example, the feminization of destitution, inconsistent portrayal in administrative roles, and boundaries to training and medical services keep on requesting regulative consideration. Perceiving and tending to these continuous difficulties is urgent for propelling a more far reaching and diverse way to deal with orientation balance.

5.1 Legislative history of the Women's Reservation Bill

The Ladies' Booking Bill, a regulative drive pointed toward upgrading ladies' political portrayal in India, has crossed an extended and mind boggling way through the country's official history. Proposing to hold 33% of all seats in the Lok Sabha (the lower place of India's Parliament) and state regulative congregations for ladies, the bill has been both an encouraging sign for orientation balance advocates and a subject of combative discussions. This investigation dives into the regulative excursion of the Ladies' Booking Bill, taking apart the achievements, challenges, and the more extensive socio-political setting that has formed its direction.

1. **Beginning of the Bill:**
The underlying foundations of the Ladies' Booking Bill can be followed back to the mid 1990s when the Panchayati Raj (Augmentation to Planned Regions) Act was ordered, saving seats for ladies in nearby administration bodies. The progress of this trial in improving ladies' support at the grassroots level gave force to a comparable drive at the public and state regulative levels.

2. **The Primary Endeavor:**
The primary authority endeavor to present the Ladies' Booking Bill at the

public level happened in September 1996 when the Deve Gowda government postponed it in the Lok Sabha. Be that as it may, the bill confronted firm resistance, with parliamentarians raising worries about its expected effect on political elements, power structures, and the rule of meritocracy.

3. **The 84th Established Alteration:**
   The energy for the bill got some decent momentum in 2008 when the UPA government, drove by Top state leader Manmohan Singh, prevailed with regards to passing the 84th Sacred Alteration Bill. This noteworthy revision looked to save 33% of the seats in the Lok Sabha and state authoritative congregations for ladies. Notwithstanding, its execution was dependent upon the entry of the Ladies' Booking Bill.

4. **Parliamentary Show and Obstacle:**
   Regardless of the section of the protected revision, the Ladies' Booking Bill kept on confronting fervent resistance when it was once again introduced in the Rajya Sabha (the upper place of Parliament) in 2010. The postponing of the bill prompted emotional scenes in the Parliament, for certain individuals tearing duplicates of the bill and taking part in uncontrollable way of behaving. The resistance was established in worries about the potential sidelining of male pioneers and the requirement for a more extensive way to deal with address ladies' issues.

5. **Interest for Quantities Inside Portions:**
   Inside the discussions encompassing the Ladies' Booking Bill, an interest arose for quantities inside standards to guarantee portrayal for underestimated networks of ladies. Pundits contended that without such arrangements, the advantages of the bill would lopsidedly build to ladies from special foundations. This request added layers of intricacy to a generally argumentative authoritative scene.

6. **Job of Common Society and Activism:**
   Common society assumed a vital part in supporting for the Ladies' Booking Bill. Ladies' associations, activists, and residents activated help, coordinated dissents, and participated in missions to push for the bill's section. The voices starting from the earliest stage to the intensification of the direness and significance of improving ladies' political portrayal.

7. **Slowed down Progress and Passed Bills:**
   Notwithstanding inconsistent endeavors to resuscitate the bill, ensuing states wrestled with the difficulties of building agreement. The bill slipped by various times because of the disintegration of Parliament without its section. The powerlessness to get cross-party support, combined with profoundly dug in resistance, obstructed the bill's advancement.

8. **Changing Political Scenes:**
   The destiny of the Ladies' Booking Bill has been unpredictably attached to the moving political scenes in India. Changes in government, philosophical realignments, and shifting needs have affected the bill's unmistakable quality on

the regulative plan. The bill frequently confronted transfer while other major problems became the overwhelming focus.

9. **Ensuing Endeavors and Passes:**
Ensuing state run administrations, including the NDA drove by State leader Narendra Modi, made endeavors to once again introduce the Ladies' Booking Bill. Nonetheless, the bill kept on slipping by without getting the important help for section. The difficulties of earning agreement across ideological groups and tending to the worries of different groups inside Parliament stayed impressive.

10. **The Street Ahead:**
As of the latest turns of events, the destiny of the Ladies' Booking Bill stays unsure. While occasional conversations and confirmations from political pioneers demonstrate an acknowledgment of the requirement for upgraded ladies' portrayal, the way ahead is loaded down with intricacies. More extensive inquiries regarding the idea of political strengthening, cultural mentalities toward ladies in administration, and the complexities of governmental policy regarding minorities in society continue.

11. **Difficulties and Resistance:**
The resistance to the Ladies' Booking Bill originates from a bunch of elements. A few pundits contend that political portrayal ought to be exclusively merit-based, communicating worries about the possible choice of competitors in view of orientation as opposed to capabilities. Others fight that the bill doesn't enough address the multifacetedness of ladies' encounters, stressing the requirement for a more comprehensive methodology.

12. **Global Correlations:**
The worldwide scene gives fascinating equals and differentiations. Numerous nations have effectively executed orientation portions in political portrayal, bringing about substantial expansions in ladies' support. Notwithstanding, the Indian experience highlights the exceptional difficulties presented by its assorted socio-social texture, complex political elements, and the profoundly dug in man centric standards.

13. **Expected Effects:**
Advocates of the Ladies' Booking Bill contend that expanded ladies' portrayal in governmental issues would have sweeping positive effects. Advocates battle that ladies bring exceptional viewpoints, needs, and initiative styles that can add to more comprehensive and responsive administration. Furthermore, improved political portrayal is viewed as a vital stage toward testing orientation based separation and cultivating cultural change.

14. **The Requirement for Complete Changes:**

The Ladies' Booking Bill, while a critical regulative drive, is essential for a more extensive structure expected for far reaching orientation equity. Legitimate measures should be supplemented by friendly and social movements, instructive changes, and financial strengthening drives to address the diverse difficulties ladies face in Indian culture.

5.2 Attempts to pass the bill

The strenuous excursion of the Ladies' Booking Bill in India has been set apart by a progression of endeavors to get its entry, each loaded with complex political elements, resistance, and difficulties. The bill, which plans to save 33% of seats in the Lok Sabha (the lower place of Parliament) and state regulative congregations for ladies, has been a point of convergence in the more extensive talk on orientation balance and political portrayal. This investigation follows the endeavors to pass the Ladies' Booking Bill, revealing insight into the complexities of every work and the variables that have added to its delayed administrative battle.

1. **The Underlying Endeavors:**
   The underlying endeavors to present the Ladies' Booking Bill in the last part of the 1990s confronted fervent resistance in the Parliament. In 1996, during the residency of State head H.D. Deve Gowda, the bill was first presented in the Lok Sabha. Be that as it may, it experienced savage opposition from a few political quarters, with pundits raising worries about its possible effect on existing power structures and the rule of meritocracy. The bill passed without being put to cast a ballot.

2. **The Unified Moderate Collusion (UPA) Time:**
   The energy for the Ladies' Booking Bill got momentum during the Unified Moderate Collusion (UPA) government's residency. In 2008, the public authority effectively passed the 84th Protected Alteration Bill, which proposed to save 33% of seats in the Lok Sabha and state authoritative congregations for ladies. This protected revision, a milestone accomplishment, was an antecedent to the Ladies' Booking Bill and meant to make the vital established system for its execution.

3. **Sensational Scenes in Parliament (2010):**
   The year 2010 saw a recharged work to pass the Ladies' Booking Bill in the Rajya Sabha. The bill's renewed introduction prompted emotional scenes in Parliament, for certain individuals tearing duplicates of the bill and taking part in boisterous way of behaving. The resistance to the bill was complex, enveloping worries about the potential sidelining of male pioneers, the requirement for a more far reaching way to deal with ladies' issues, and the interest for quantities inside standards to address the portrayal of minimized networks of ladies.

4. **Shares Inside Portions Debate:**
   The interest for shares inside portions added a layer of intricacy to the regulative talk encompassing the Ladies' Booking Bill. Pundits contended that without arrangements to guarantee portrayal for minimized networks of ladies, the advantages of the bill would lopsidedly build to ladies from special foundations.

This discussion further strengthened the discussions inside Parliament and added to the bill's extended official excursion.

5. **Slowed down Progress and Passed Bills:**
In spite of the section of the 84th Sacred Correction and irregular endeavors to once again introduce the Ladies' Booking Bill, progress remained slowed down. The bill slipped by different times because of the disintegration of Parliament without its section. The failure to get cross-party support, combined with profoundly settled in resistance, blocked the bill's advancement and left its destiny dubious.

6. **Changing Political Scenes:**
The destiny of the Ladies' Booking Bill has been intently attached to the moving political scenes in India. Changes in government, philosophical realignments, and fluctuating needs have impacted the bill's noticeable quality on the administrative plan. The bill frequently confronted assignment while other major problems became the dominant focal point, mirroring the perplexing transaction between political elements and official needs.

7. **Resulting Endeavors and Passes:**
Resulting states, including the Public Vote based Coalition (NDA) drove by State leader Narendra Modi, made endeavors to once again introduce the Ladies' Booking Bill. Nonetheless, the bill kept on slipping by without getting the essential help for entry. The difficulties of earning agreement across ideological groups and tending to the worries of different groups inside Parliament stayed imposing, adding to the bill's administrative misfortunes.

8. **Job of Common Society and Activism:**
All through the endeavors to pass the Ladies' Booking Bill, common society assumed a vital part in pushing for its section. Ladies' associations, activists, and residents activated help, coordinated dissents, and participated in missions to push for the bill's section. The grassroots preparation highlighted the earnestness and significance of upgrading ladies' political portrayal, adding to the enhancement of the bill as a critical instrument for orientation balance.

9. **Worldwide Examinations:**
Global encounters with orientation quantities in political portrayal give fascinating equals and differentiations. Numerous nations have effectively executed such measures, bringing about substantial expansions in ladies' cooperation in governmental issues. In any case, the Indian experience highlights the special difficulties presented by its assorted socio-social texture, complex political elements, and profoundly settled in male centric standards.

10. **Difficulties and Resistance:**
The Ladies' Booking Bill has experienced diverse resistance, mirroring the intricacy of the issues in question. A few pundits contend that political portrayal ought to be exclusively merit-based, communicating worries about the expected determination of competitors in view of orientation as opposed to capabilities.

Others battle that the bill doesn't sufficiently address the diversity of ladies' encounters, underlining the requirement for a more comprehensive methodology.

11. **Expected Effects:**

   Advocates of the Ladies' Booking Bill contend that expanded ladies' portrayal in governmental issues would have extensive positive effects. Advocates fight that ladies bring one of a kind viewpoints, needs, and initiative styles that can add to more comprehensive and responsive administration. Moreover, improved political portrayal is viewed as a pivotal move toward testing orientation based segregation and cultivating cultural change.

12. **The Requirement for Extensive Changes:**

   While the Ladies' Booking Bill is a huge regulative drive, it is essential for a more extensive structure expected for thorough orientation uniformity. Lawful measures should be supplemented by friendly and social movements, instructive changes, and financial strengthening drives to address the complex difficulties ladies face in Indian culture. The bill, whenever ordered, could act as an impetus for more extensive cultural changes, testing orientation standards and reshaping political scenes.

13. **The Street Ahead:**

As of the latest turns of events, the destiny of the Ladies' Booking Bill stays unsure. Occasional conversations and confirmations from political pioneers show an acknowledgment of the requirement for improved ladies' portrayal, yet the way ahead is weighed down with intricacies. More extensive inquiries concerning the idea of political strengthening, cultural perspectives toward ladies in administration, and the complexities of governmental policy regarding minorities in society endure.

5.3 Challenges and setbacks faced in the legislative process

The regulative excursion of the Ladies' Booking Bill in India has been loaded with various difficulties and misfortunes, mirroring the complex and frequently petulant nature of endeavors to upgrade ladies' portrayal in governmental issues. While the bill holds the commitment of breaking conventional orientation standards and cultivating more prominent inclusivity, its advancement has been hindered by a huge number of variables going from political resistance to profoundly instilled man centric standards. This investigation digs into the difficulties and misfortunes looked by the Ladies' Booking Bill all through its official cycle.

1. **Political Resistance and Hesitance:**

   One of the essential difficulties looked by the Ladies' Booking Bill has been political resistance and hesitance among different political groups. A few political pioneers, especially those having a place with male-overwhelmed parties, have opposed the possibility of ladies' booking, seeing it as a danger to existing power structures. The hesitance to surrender space to ladies in governmental issues has appeared in discussions and conversations inside Parliament, frequently prompting slowed down progress and deferred navigation.

2. **Protection from Amounts Inside Shares:**
The interest for portions inside shares, pointed toward guaranteeing portrayal for minimized networks of ladies, has been a disagreeable issue. While advocates contend that such arrangements are fundamental for address interconnection and keep the bill from excessively helping ladies from special foundations, rivals fight that it confounds the administrative scene. This inside division has added to an absence of agreement and further impeded the bill's entry.

3. **Intra-Party Resistance:**
Resistance to the Ladies' Booking Bill isn't bound to between party elements; it additionally reaches out inside ideological groups. Some party individuals have communicated contradict, seeing the bill as a takeoff from merit-based choice and a burden of standards. Intra-party divisions make difficulties in introducing a brought together front, and clashing sentiments inside gatherings can prompt inward strains and discussions.

4. **Absence of Cross-Party Agreement:**
Accomplishing cross-party agreement on the Ladies' Booking Bill has shown to be an impressive test. The bill needs expansive based help to get the important decisions in favor of entry, yet political contrasts and contending needs have impeded the development of a bound together front. In a different and multi-party political scene like India, collecting agreement on a disagreeable issue, for example, ladies' booking turns out to be progressively difficult.

5. **Confusions and Generalizations:**
The regulative cycle has been damaged by confusions and generalizations encompassing ladies' abilities in political authority. A few pundits contend that the bill could prompt the choice of ladies exclusively founded on orientation as opposed to capabilities, sustaining the idea that ladies are less able or experienced in political issues. Conquering profoundly instilled orientation inclinations and testing generalizations stays a huge obstacle.

6. **Protection from Governmental policy regarding minorities in society:**
The Ladies' Booking Bill addresses a type of governmental policy regarding minorities in society intended to address verifiable orientation based imbalances. Be that as it may, protection from governmental policy regarding minorities in society, even as orientation standards, continues. Some contend that political portrayal ought to be altogether merit-based, disregarding the fundamental obstructions and inclinations that have generally barred ladies from political support. The protection from governmental policy regarding minorities in society represents a key test to the bill's acknowledgment.

7. **Social and Social Backfire:**
The social and social texture of Indian culture assumes a vital part in forming perspectives toward ladies' cooperation in governmental issues. Customary

orientation jobs and well established male centric standards add to a social reaction against the possibility of ladies possessing a critical extent of political seats. Changing cultural perspectives requires regulative measures as well as more extensive social moves that challenge profoundly instilled orientation generalizations.

8. **Challenges in Executing Standards:**
Regardless of whether the Ladies' Booking Bill were to pass, challenges in executing standards at the ground level represent a critical obstruction. Guaranteeing that ideological groups conform to the booking standards, beating obstruction inside party structures, and resolving calculated issues connected with up-and-comer choice and revolution require cautious preparation and observing. The compelling execution of standards is vital for the bill's prosperity.

9. **Absence of Far reaching Changes:**
While the Ladies' Booking Bill is a critical stage toward orientation fairness in political portrayal, it's anything but a panacea for the multi-layered difficulties ladies face in Indian culture. The absence of complete changes resolving issues like schooling, monetary strengthening, and social mentalities restricts the bill's possible effect. An all encompassing methodology that joins regulative measures with more extensive cultural changes is fundamental for extraordinary orientation equity.

10. **Multifacetedness and Minimization:**
The bill has confronted analysis for not enough tending to interconnection and the particular difficulties looked by minimized networks of ladies. The interest for standards inside amounts highlights the need to consider the assorted encounters of ladies from various financial, position, and strict foundations. Inability to address these worries has prompted divisions inside the promotion for the bill.

11. **Absence of Public Mindfulness and Training:**
The progress of the Ladies' Booking Bill is complicatedly connected to public mindfulness and comprehension of its importance. The absence of broad mindfulness about the bill's goals, the significance of ladies' portrayal, and the likely advantages for administration ruins its acknowledgment. Instructive drives and mindfulness crusades are crucial for assemble public help for regulative measures advancing orientation equity.

12. **Financial Variations and Political Impact:**
Financial abberations and the impact of monetary power in governmental issues present difficulties to the Ladies' Booking Bill. Ladies from financially special foundations might in any case enjoy an unbalanced benefit with regards to political impact and admittance to assets. Crossing over financial variations and tending to the job of cash in legislative issues are pivotal parts of guaranteeing fair political portrayal.

13. **Worldwide Points of reference and Social Responsiveness:**

While worldwide points of reference exhibit effective executions of orientation portions, the Indian setting requires a nuanced comprehension of social responsiveness. The variety of India's social and provincial scenes requires a methodology that regards nearby subtleties and customs while making progress toward orientation uniformity. Offsetting worldwide prescribed procedures with social responsiveness represents a continuous test in outlining and advancing such regulation.

Chapter 6

Success Stories from Reservations

In the midst of the difficulties and discussions encompassing bookings for ladies in India, there are convincing examples of overcoming adversity that highlight the extraordinary effect of expanded female portrayal in different circles. These examples of overcoming adversity act as guides of progress, representing the positive results that can arise whenever ladies are given equivalent open doors and a stage to feature their capacities. This investigation digs into examples of overcoming adversity from reservations in India, revealing insight into how governmental policy regarding minorities in society has catalyzed positive changes in legislative issues, administration, and cultural discernments.

1. **Political Strengthening:**
   One of the striking examples of overcoming adversity emerging from reservations is the expanded political strengthening of ladies. In locales where ladies have been chosen for held seats, there has been an unmistakable change in political elements. Ladies pioneers have effectively added to strategy detailing, supported for orientation delicate regulation, and resolved issues influencing underestimated networks.

   The groundbreaking force of political portrayal is exemplified by the way that ladies chiefs frequently focus on issues like instruction, medical services, and social government assistance, subsequently encouraging a more comprehensive and all encompassing way to deal with administration.

2. **Successful Neighborhood Administration:**
   Reservations play had a significant impact in upgrading the viability of nearby administration. Ladies chose for saved seats in Panchayati Raj organizations have been instrumental in advancing grassroots turn of events. Their authority has prompted drives zeroing in on sterilization, medical services, and training, lining up with the more extensive objective of practical and fair local area improvement. The accentuation on neighborhood administration has demonstrated to

be an impetus for positive change, as ladies pioneers carry novel viewpoints that reverberate with the requirements of their networks.

3. **Breaking Orientation Generalizations:**
   Reservations have been instrumental in testing and breaking customary orientation generalizations. Ladies who climb to strategic, influential places through reservations act as good examples, testing assumptions about the jobs and capacities of ladies in the public eye. This change in discernment has a flowing impact, motivating more youthful ages and cultivating a more comprehensive and orientation delicate cultural viewpoint. As ladies expect different jobs in administration, they add to destroying dug in predispositions and making ready for a more evenhanded society.

4. **Worked on Instructive Fulfillment:**
   Reservations have added to a positive connection between's expanded female political portrayal and worked on instructive results. Ladies pioneers, mindful of the extraordinary capability of training, have advocated drives that focus on admittance to quality schooling for young ladies. This emphasis on schooling as a principal right lines up with more extensive improvement objectives and cultivates a favorable climate for the strengthening of people in the future.

5. **Medical services Drives:**
   Ladies pioneers in held seats have been at the very front of upholding for and carrying out medical services drives. Perceiving the diversity of orientation and wellbeing, these pioneers have advocated programs tending to maternal wellbeing, family arranging, and medical services availability. Their impact reaches out past conventional political areas, as they effectively draw in with networks to bring issues to light about medical problems and scaffold holes in medical services arrangement.

6. **Financial Strengthening:**
   Reservations have worked with financial strengthening by giving ladies a stage to impact strategies that straightforwardly influence monetary turn of events. Ladies pioneers in held seats have pushed for monetary drives, for example, ability improvement programs, microfinance valuable open doors, and business venture support, adding to the monetary freedom of ladies in their voting demographics. This financial strengthening, thus, meaningfully affects cultural designs and adds to the by and large monetary development of networks.

7. **Local area Improvement and Civil rights:**
   The effect of reservations reaches out past individual examples of overcoming adversity to include more extensive local area improvement and civil rights drives. Ladies pioneers, frequently more sensitive to the necessities of minimized networks, have been instrumental in upholding for the freedoms of socially and monetarily burdened gatherings. Their portrayal has prompted strategies resolving issues of land freedoms, social consideration, and admittance to assets, in this way encouraging an all the more and impartial society.

8. **Diminishing Orientation Based Viciousness:**
   Expanded female portrayal has been connected to a decrease in orientation based savagery. Ladies pioneers in held situates effectively participate in drives to bring issues to light about orientation based viciousness, advocate for lawful measures, and make encouraging groups of people for survivors. Their presence in places of impact adds to changing cultural perspectives and testing the standardization of viciousness against ladies, making more secure spaces for ladies in both public and confidential circles.

9. **Advancement of Ladies' Freedoms:**
   Reservations have been instrumental in propelling ladies' freedoms by enhancing the voices of ladies pioneers who effectively champion orientation touchy regulation. Ladies in saved seats have been at the very front of upholding for legitimate measures resolving issues like aggressive behavior at home, work environment badgering, and conceptive privileges. Their support adds to forming a lawful system that lines up with the standards of uniformity and equity.

10. **Moving People in the future:**
    The examples of overcoming adversity arising out of reservations act as strong stories that move and persuade people in the future of ladies. As little kids observer ladies pioneers breaking hindrances and making significant commitments to their networks, they are urged to seek to places of authority. This optimistic shift is essential in destroying fundamental obstructions and cultivating a culture where ladies' support in administration is standardized.

11. **Improved Social Union:**
    Reservations have added to improved social union by cultivating comprehensive administration. Ladies pioneers, by ethicalness of their expanded portrayal, carry assorted viewpoints and encounters to dynamic cycles. This variety of thought and portrayal adds to a more comprehensive and participatory administration model, where the requirements and desires of all sections of society are considered.

12. **Affirmation of Multifacetedness:**
    The examples of overcoming adversity from reservations highlight the significance of recognizing multifacetedness in policymaking. Ladies pioneers from assorted foundations, including those from minimized networks, feature the requirement for approaches that think about the layered encounters of ladies. Reservations give a system to guaranteeing that the voices of ladies with crossing characters are not minimized however effectively add to molding strategies that address their novel difficulties.

13. **Rising above Political Walkways:**

The examples of overcoming adversity from reservations exhibit that the effect of expanded female portrayal rises above political paths. Ladies pioneers have shown an ability to team up across partisan loyalties on issues that significantly affect the prosperity of networks. This cooperative soul adds to a more practical and helpful world of politics, where shared objectives outweigh sectarian divisions.

6.1 Women who benefited from reservations

The execution of bookings for ladies in India has introduced another time of chances, breaking conventional obstructions and giving a stage to ladies to take part in governmental issues and administration effectively. The accounts of ladies who have profited from reservations act as strong stories of strength, initiative, and ground-breaking change. In this investigation, we dig into the assorted encounters of ladies who have profited from reservations, delineating the complex effect of governmental policy regarding minorities in society on their lives and the more extensive networks they address.

1. **Administration in Panchayati Raj Establishments:**
   One of the critical regions where ladies have profited from reservations is in Panchayati Raj establishments. These foundations, which structure the foundation of rustic administration, have seen a prominent expansion in the support of ladies pioneers in held seats. Ladies who have rose to places of Sarpanch or other influential positions in Gram Panchayats play had a critical impact in molding neighborhood strategies, tending to local area needs, and pushing for comprehensive turn of events.

   Take, for instance, the tale of Sunita, a lady from a provincial town in Rajasthan, who challenged and won the place of Sarpanch through a held seat. Sunita, in spite of confronting starting doubt, exhibited successful administration by focusing on drives connected with training, medical care, and sterilization in her town. Through her residency, she worked on nearby framework as well as motivated different ladies locally to participate in the majority rule process effectively.

2. **Political Pioneers in State Gatherings:**
   Bookings for ladies stretch out past neighborhood administration to state authoritative congregations. Ladies who have profited from saved seats in state congregations have been instrumental in molding territorial arrangements and pushing for issues that reverberate with assorted bodies electorate. These ladies explore the mind boggling landscape of state legislative issues, testing orientation standards and making ready for more prominent portrayal at higher echelons of force.

   An illustrative model is the narrative of Anuradha, who, through a saved seat, turned into an Individual from the Regulative Get together (MLA) in a northern province of India. Anuradha has been a vocal supporter for ladies' freedoms, instruction, and medical services. Her presence in the state gathering has added to the enhancement of ladies' voices and the presentation of regulation pointed toward tending to orientation based abberations.

3. **Instructive Strengthening Supporters:**
Bookings for ladies have likewise assumed a vital part in hoisting ladies as supporters for instructive strengthening. Ladies pioneers who have profited from saved situates frequently focus on drives pointed toward further developing admittance to quality instruction, especially for young ladies. Their support reaches out past the limits of political foundations, impacting instructive strategies and encouraging a culture of advancing inside their voting public.
Consider the instance of Kavita, a lady chief in a semi-metropolitan electorate, who used her situation in the nearby government to support instructive changes. Kavita's attention on building schools, guaranteeing the accessibility of qualified educators, and upholding for grants has fundamentally added to worked on instructive results locally.

4. **Business venture and Monetary Drives:**
Bookings for ladies have opened ways to political initiative as well as catalyzed monetary strengthening. Ladies pioneers who have profited from reservations frequently channel their impact to advance business, monetary drives, and monetary consideration inside their networks. Their endeavors add to breaking financial hindrances and encouraging monetary independence.
A moving model is the narrative of Nandini, a lady chief in an ancestral district, who utilized her saved seat to advocate for monetary drives. Nandini worked with ability advancement programs, microfinance open doors, and market linkages for ladies in her voting public, enabling them to begin their own organizations and add to the nearby economy.

5. **Champions for Medical care and Disinfection:**
Ladies pioneers in saved seats have arisen as champions for medical care and disinfection drives. Their impact stretches out to molding strategies that address basic medical problems, advance cleanliness, and guarantee admittance to medical services administrations.
By focusing on these issues, ladies pioneers add to the general prosperity and wellbeing results of their networks.
Take the case of Priya, a lady chief from a rustic electorate, who utilized her situation to advocate for further developed medical care framework. Priya's drives went from coordinating wellbeing camps to pushing for the development of medical services offices in underserved regions. Her endeavors lastingly affect the wellbeing and prosperity of the local area individuals.

6. **Advocates for Civil rights and Minimized People group:**
Ladies pioneers who have profited from reservations frequently arise as backers for civil rights, effectively attempting to address the requirements of underestimated networks. By excellence of their positions, they enhance the voices of the people who have been generally minimized and advocate for strategies that advance inclusivity and value.
Consider the narrative of Ayesha, a lady chief from a minority local area, who

used her saved seat to address the worries of minimized gatherings. Ayesha's support spread over issues connected with land freedoms, social consideration, and admittance to government plans, adding to an all the more and evenhanded society.

7. **Media and Support:**

Bookings for ladies have engaged pioneers inside conventional political circles as well as prepared for ladies to become compelling figures in media and promotion. Ladies pioneers who have profited from reservations frequently utilize their situations to bring issues to light about basic issues, challenge cultural standards, and backer for moderate change through different media stages.

An illustrative model is the tale of Radhika, a lady chief who changed from legislative issues to media after her residency in a saved seat. Radhika currently has a well known TV program where she examines squeezing social issues, advocates for orientation correspondence, and intensifies the voices of minimized networks.

8. **Social and Social Powerhouses:**

Past formal political designs, ladies who have profited from reservations frequently become social and social powerhouses. Their initiative rises above conventional jobs, testing generalizations and reshaping cultural accounts about the job of ladies. These ladies become images of strengthening, affecting cultural mentalities and rousing others to seek after influential positions.

The tale of Meera, a lady chief from a metropolitan body electorate, epitomizes this direction. Meera's impact reaches out past her political obligations; she effectively draws in with local area occasions, social drives, and social missions, testing orientation standards and adding to a more comprehensive and moderate social scene.

9. **Engaging People in the future:**

Maybe one of the most significant results of bookings for ladies is the strengthening of people in the future. Ladies pioneers who have profited from held seats become pioneers, moving little kids to seek to places of authority. The effect of this motivation is significant, cultivating a generational change in mentalities towards orientation jobs and capacities.

Consider the tale of Divya, a lady chief who effectively draws in with schools and universities in her supporters. Divya's endeavors incorporate coaching little kids, sorting out authority studios, and upholding for instructive changes that engage the up and coming age of ladies to take part in administration and initiative effectively.

10. **Making a More Comprehensive Political Scene:**

The tales of ladies who have profited from reservations by and large add to the making of a more comprehensive political scene. By effectively taking part in governmental issues and administration, these ladies challenge the verifiable underrepresentation of ladies in dynamic cycles. Their presence encourages a more different and delegate political circle, mirroring the wealth of viewpoints and encounters inside the more extensive populace.

An all-encompassing subject across these different stories is the extraordinary effect of bookings for ladies. While every account is exceptional, on the whole, they underline the catalyzing impact of governmental policy regarding minorities in society in destroying foundational boundaries, encouraging inclusivity, and establishing a climate where ladies can flourish as pioneers, supporters, and impetuses for positive change.

6.2 Political success stories

The execution of bookings for ladies in India has proclaimed another period of political strengthening, delivering a partner of dynamic ladies pioneers who have explored the complicated territory of legislative issues, tested orientation standards, and made a permanent imprint on the country's political scene. These political examples of overcoming adversity highlight the extraordinary effect of governmental policy regarding minorities in society, exhibiting how expanded female portrayal adds to more comprehensive and responsive administration. In this investigation, we dig into the assorted and rousing political examples of overcoming adversity of ladies who have ascended to unmistakable quality through held seats, molding arrangements, supporting for change, and breaking obstructions simultaneously.

1. **Administration in Neighborhood Administration:**
   Ladies pioneers who have climbed to situate in neighborhood administration through held seats play had a vital impact in reshaping local area elements. One outstanding example of overcoming adversity is that of Ananya, who turned into the top of her Gram Panchayat through a held seat.
   Ananya zeroed in on grassroots turn of events, focusing on drives connected with schooling, medical services, and framework. Her initiative carried substantial enhancements to her town as well as roused another age of ladies to take part in nearby administration effectively.
   Ananya's prosperity is significant of the more extensive effect of expanded female portrayal in neighborhood administration, where ladies pioneers carry an exceptional point of view to address the prompt necessities of their networks, cultivating a more comprehensive and participatory type of administration.

2. **State Authoritative Victories:**
   The effect of reservations reaches out past neighborhood administration to state regulative congregations, where ladies pioneers have cut out a space for them and pushed for strategies that resound with different electorates. A brilliant illustration is the political excursion of Rukmini, who, through a saved seat, turned into an Individual from the Regulative Gathering (MLA) in a southern state.
   Rukmini's residency saw her dynamic commitment to regulations tending to ladies' freedoms, training, and medical care. Her prosperity features the critical

job that saved seats play in giving a stage to ladies to impact provincial strategies and add to the more extensive political talk.

3. **Public Portrayal in Parliament:**

   Held seats have additionally prepared for ladies to accomplish public portrayal in the Parliament, the most elevated administrative body in India. The example of overcoming adversity of Aisha, who turned into an Individual from Parliament (MP) through a saved seat, epitomizes the more extensive effect of ladies' political cooperation at the public level.

   Aisha, during her residency, effectively supported for orientation touchy regulation, monetary strengthening, and civil rights. Her excursion grandstands how governmental policy regarding minorities in society in legislative issues can prompt a more different and comprehensive public council, guaranteeing that the voices of ladies are essential to the regulative cycle at the most elevated echelons of force.

4. **Multifacetedness and Promotion:**

   Ladies pioneers who have profited from reservations frequently carry a nuanced comprehension of multifacetedness to their promotion. Such pioneers effectively champion the freedoms of minimized networks, resolving issues of station, religion, and financial abberations. The tale of Maya, a lady chief from a generally underestimated local area, epitomizes this diverse promotion.

   Maya involved her situation in neighborhood administration to advocate for land freedoms, social consideration, and admittance to government plans for her local area. Her prosperity features the job of saved seats in guaranteeing that the political scene mirrors the variety of India's socio-social texture.

5. **Support for Ladies' Privileges:**

   Saved seats have been instrumental in raising voices that promoter for ladies' privileges inside the political circle. Ladies pioneers like Shruti have used their situations to effectively advocate issues connected with orientation uniformity, conceptive freedoms, and lawful changes. Shruti's support inside the state assembly added to the entry of regulations tending to abusive behavior at home and working environment provocation.

   The outcome of ladies pioneers like Shruti mirrors the more extensive effect of governmental policy regarding minorities in society in establishing a more orientation delicate regulative climate, where strategies are molded to address the novel difficulties looked by ladies.

6. **Key Job in Navigation:**

   Ladies who have profited from reservations frequently assume an essential part in dynamic cycles, impacting strategies that lastingly affect their supporters. Radhika, a lady chief who rose to noticeable quality through a held seat, effectively participated in councils and subcommittees, contributing her experiences to shape official choices.

   Radhika's story epitomizes how ladies' cooperation in dynamic cycles can prompt more exhaustive and all around informed arrangements, guaranteeing that assorted points of view are considered in the plan of regulations and guidelines.

7. **Inventive Approach Drives:**

Governmental policy regarding minorities in society in legislative issues has worked with the execution of imaginative approach drives by ladies pioneers. The example of overcoming adversity of Neha, a civil councilor who accomplished her situation through a saved seat, features her endeavors to present strategies that emphasis on practical turn of events, squander the board, and metropolitan preparation.

Neha's drives changed her district as well as turned into a model for different locales. Saved seats, by giving ladies the chance to lead, add to the development of inventive and ground breaking approaches that address the advancing requirements of networks.

8. **Worldwide Portrayal and Strategy:**

The effect of expanded female portrayal through held seats stretches out to the worldwide field, where ladies pioneers effectively participate in discretionary endeavors and address India on global stages. The example of overcoming adversity of Priya, who changed from a saved seat to a discretionary job, represents the worldwide impact of ladies pioneers.

Priya's job in worldwide strategy displayed the potential for ladies pioneers to address India on a worldwide scale, adding to political endeavors, advancing respective relations, and supporting for worldwide drives that line up with India's inclinations.

9. **Local area Building and Grassroots Commitment:**

Held seats engage ladies pioneers to draw in with their networks, building extensions and cultivating grassroots improvement effectively. The tale of Ayesha, who arose as a pioneer through a saved seat, features her obligation to local area building. Ayesha effectively draws in with nearby drives, addresses local area concerns, and makes stages for discourse among occupants and policymakers.

Ayesha's prosperity shows the way that ladies chiefs, through saved seats, can become impetuses for positive change at the grassroots level, guaranteeing that arrangements line up with the necessities and goals of the networks they serve.

10. **Changing Public Discernments:**

Ladies pioneers who have ascended to unmistakable quality through held seats add to changing public discernments about the job of ladies in governmental issues. Their examples of overcoming adversity challenge conventional thoughts and generalizations, making a story where ladies are viewed as proficient and successful pioneers. The tale of Meera, a lady chief from a metropolitan body electorate, epitomizes this extraordinary effect.

11. **Backing for Maintainable Turn of events:**

Ladies pioneers in held situates frequently advocate for maintainable turn of events, accentuating natural preservation, sustainable power, and eco-accommodating strategies. The example of overcoming adversity of Tanvi, a forerunner in a locale committee, exhibits her obligation to manageability drives. Through her administration, Tanvi initiated projects that zeroed in on natural preservation, squander decrease, and advancing eco-accommodating practices.

12. **Empowering Youth Interest:**

Ladies pioneers who have profited from saved situates effectively support youth cooperation in governmental issues, encouraging the up and coming age of pioneers. The tale of Divya, a metropolitan councilor, features her endeavors to draw in with schools and universities in her voting public. Divya coaches youthful people, sorts out administration studios, and promoters for instructive changes that enable the adolescent to partake in administration effectively.

6.3 Economic and social impact on reserved constituencies

The execution of bookings for ladies in political voting demographics in India has reshaped the political scene as well as created critical monetary and social effects inside these held electorates.

The mixture of ladies into political administrative roles through reservations has achieved extraordinary changes, encouraging financial turn of events, social strengthening, and a redefinition of conventional orientation jobs. In this investigation, we dive into the financial and social effect of saved bodies electorate, analyzing how expanded female portrayal has converted into unmistakable advantages for networks.

1. **Monetary Strengthening Through Business:**
   One of the prominent financial effects of held electorates is the advancement of business venture among ladies. Ladies pioneers who have climbed to political situations through saved situates frequently champion monetary drives that engage ladies monetarily. These drives range from expertise advancement projects to the foundation of miniature endeavors and self improvement gatherings.
   For example, in a saved supporters in provincial Maharashtra, a lady chief named Priya led a progression of monetary strengthening programs. Through her endeavors, ladies in the electorate got preparing in different professional abilities, prompting the foundation of private ventures and bungalow enterprises. This monetary strengthening not just superior the monetary remaining of individual families yet additionally added to the generally speaking financial improvement of the local area.

2. **Framework Advancement and Business Amazing open doors:**
   Saved electorates have seen a flood in framework improvement projects under the initiative of ladies delegates. These pioneers effectively advocate for and distribute assets to work on nearby foundation, including streets, schools, medical services offices, and disinfection. The inception of such ventures not just

upgrades the personal satisfaction for occupants yet additionally sets out work open doors inside the supporters.

An illustrative model is the held voting public of Sonali, where the lady chief, through essential designation of assets, focused on the development of local area framework. This tended to well established infrastructural holes as well as produced business potential open doors for nearby occupants, animating monetary development inside the voting public.

3. **Center around Instruction and Ability Improvement:**

   Ladies pioneers in saved bodies electorate frequently focus on training and expertise improvement drives, perceiving the groundbreaking effect of schooling on individual lives and local area advancement. By pushing for instructive changes, laying out schools, and supporting expertise improvement programs, these pioneers add to making a more taught and gifted labor force.

   In a held electorate in Uttar Pradesh, a lady chief named Aarti supported instructive drives pointed toward further developing admittance to quality training for young ladies. Aarti's endeavors expanded school enlistment among young ladies as well as made ready for expertise improvement programs, upgrading the employability of youthful people in the voting public.

4. **Medical services Access and Drives:**

   Held voting demographics have encountered better medical services access and drives under the authority of ladies delegates. Ladies pioneers frequently focus on medical care framework, advocate for wellbeing mindfulness projects, and work towards decreasing wellbeing inconsistencies inside their voting demographics.

   Think about the held voting public of Meena, where the lady chief effectively taken part in medical care drives. Through her endeavors, Meena worked with the foundation of medical services centers, coordinated wellbeing camps, and pushed for better medical services offices. The outcome was a huge improvement in medical care results and a decrease in preventable sicknesses inside the supporters.

5. **Strengthening of Minimized People group:**

   One of the social effects of held voting public is the strengthening of minimized networks, as ladies pioneers effectively advocate for their privileges and address verifiable treacheries. Held situates frequently give a stage to ladies pioneers from underestimated foundations to address their networks and address social differences.

   In a saved voting demographic in Bihar, a lady chief named Anjali, having a place with a generally minimized local area, arose as a strong promoter for civil rights. Anjali's initiative prompted strategies tending to land privileges, admittance to assets, and social consideration, enabling minimized networks and cultivating a more fair society.

6. **Decrease in Orientation Based Savagery:**
   The presence of ladies pioneers in held bodies electorate has been connected to a decrease in orientation based brutality. Ladies delegates frequently focus on promotion against abusive behavior at home, provocation, and segregation. Their dynamic commitment to authoritative cycles adds to the creation and fortifying of regulations pointed toward safeguarding ladies' freedoms.
   An illustrative model is the held voting public of Geeta, where the lady chief effectively supported for and executed measures to address orientation based savagery. Geeta's endeavors brought issues to light about these issues as well as added to an adjustment of cultural perspectives, encouraging a more secure and more comprehensive climate for ladies.

7. **Local area Based Projects for Social Government assistance:**
   Saved supporters have seen the execution of local area based programs for social government assistance under the authority of ladies delegates. These projects envelop many drives, including destitution easing, government managed retirement, and backing for weak populaces.
   In a held voting public in Odisha, a lady chief named Lakshmi started local area put together projects that engaged with respect to social government assistance. Lakshmi's administration prompted the execution of plans supporting underestimated gatherings, older residents, and people confronting monetary difficulties. The outcome was an improvement in the general prosperity of the local area.

8. **Support for Natural Protection:**
   Ladies pioneers in saved voting demographics frequently participate in support for ecological preservation and feasible turn of events. Perceiving the interconnectedness of natural wellbeing and local area prosperity, these pioneers champion approaches that advance eco-accommodating practices and address natural difficulties.
   A model is the saved body electorate of Ananya, where the lady chief effectively pushed for ecological protection drives. Ananya's endeavors prompted the execution of undertakings zeroed in on squander the board, afforestation, and supportable horticultural works on, adding to both monetary and ecological supportability inside the electorate.

9. **Advancement of Social Consideration and Variety:**
   Saved supporters have become stages for the advancement of social incorporation and variety, as ladies pioneers effectively work to connect holes and guarantee equivalent open doors for all sections of society. By resolving issues connected with position, religion, and identity, these pioneers add to encouraging a more comprehensive and agreeable local area.
   In a held voting public in Karnataka, a lady chief named Deepa supported drives that advanced social consideration and variety. Deepa's authority brought about

strategies tending to separation, establishing a more comprehensive climate where people from different foundations felt addressed and upheld.

10. **Advancement of Social and Imaginative Drives:**
    Ladies pioneers in saved supporters frequently add to the advancement of social and imaginative drives, perceiving the significance of safeguarding and commending the social legacy of their networks. By supporting nearby specialists, arranging widespread developments, and upholding for the protection of social practices, these pioneers add to the improvement of local area life.

11. **Engaging Ladies in Customary Occupations:**
    Saved supporters have seen drives pointed toward enabling ladies participated in conventional occupations. Ladies pioneers effectively support ladies engaged with farming, painstaking work, and other customary exchanges, giving them the vital assets and chances to improve their monetary autonomy.

12. **Youth Commitment and Interest:**

Ladies pioneers in saved voting public frequently effectively draw in with the adolescent, encouraging their cooperation in local area advancement and political cycles. Through mentorship programs, administration studios, and backing for youth-driven approaches, these pioneers add to molding the eventual fate of their electorates.

Chapter 7

Overcoming Challenges in Implementation

The execution of bookings for ladies in India, however an extraordinary strategy, has not been without its arrangement of difficulties. Defeating profoundly imbued cultural standards, obstruction from different quarters, and tending to the complexities of an assorted and complex political scene have been imposing errands. In this investigation, we dig into the difficulties looked in the execution of bookings for ladies and the techniques utilized to defeat these obstacles, pondering the continuous excursion towards a more comprehensive and delegate political framework.

1. **Cultural Opposition and Orientation Predisposition:**
   One of the essential difficulties in the execution of bookings for ladies has been cultural opposition established in firmly established orientation predisposition. Customary standards and generalizations frequently cast questions on ladies' capacities to lead, building up the idea that political initiative is a male privilege. This inclination shows among the overall people as well as inside ideological groups and foundations.
   Conquering this challenge requires a complex methodology. Sharpening efforts and mindfulness programs have been started to challenge cliché discernments about ladies' initiative capacities. Grassroots developments and common society associations assume a pivotal part in really impacting cultural outlooks by advancing stories that feature the skill and viability of ladies pioneers.
2. **Political Resistance and Reactions:**
   The execution of reservations has confronted huge political resistance and reactions from different quarters. Some contend that reservations compromise meritocracy, attesting that political pioneers ought to be chosen exclusively founded on their capacities instead of orientation. Furthermore, ideological groups, in certain occasions, have been impervious to designating held seats to ladies, frequently liking to handle male competitors in electorates with a higher probability of progress.

Tending to political resistance includes building agreement through exchange and featuring the bigger cultural advantages of expanded female portrayal. Backing gatherings and ladies' associations play had a vital impact in drawing in with political pioneers, underscoring the significance of variety in dynamic cycles. Public tension and mindfulness crusades likewise add to pushing political substances towards embracing the soul of orientation comprehensive administration.

3. **Restricted Admittance to Assets:**

Ladies competitors frequently face difficulties connected with restricted admittance to monetary assets, which frustrates their capacity to really battle. Monetary requirements, combined with the common orientation wage hole, make a lopsided battleground, making it challenging for ladies to rival male partners who could have more huge monetary support.

To resolve this issue, there have been calls for monetary changes in political crusading, including measures to give equivalent admittance to assets to both male and female applicants. A few drives incorporate the arrangement of assets explicitly reserved for ladies competitors, empowering them to lead strong and serious political races. Furthermore, limit building programs center around engaging ladies to explore raising money challenges and oversee crusade funds really.

4. **Social and Cultural Obstructions:**

Social and cultural obstructions present critical hindrances to the powerful execution of bookings for ladies. Winning standards and assumptions regarding ladies' jobs inside the family and society can deter ladies from effectively taking part in governmental issues. Social inclinations frequently sustain the conviction that ladies ought to focus on familial obligations over political pursuits.

Procedures to conquer social and cultural obstructions include local area commitment and mindfulness programs that challenge conventional standards. By displaying the positive effect of ladies pioneers on networks and tending to worries about adjusting family obligations, these drives plan to move social discernments and establish a climate helpful for ladies' dynamic support in legislative issues.

5. **Absence of Political Experience and Openness:**

Ladies up-and-comers in held bodies electorate might confront difficulties connected with an absence of political experience and openness. Restricted open doors for ladies to participate in political exercises, combined with verifiable underrepresentation, add to a deficiency of experienced ladies pioneers. This absence of involvement can be taken advantage of by rivals and may impact citizens' discernments.

To address this test, mentorship projects and administration preparing drives have been acquainted with give ladies the vital abilities and openness to explore the complexities of political authority. These projects center around building the certainty of ladies competitors, furnishing them with the information and apparatuses expected to participate in political cycles really.

6. **Party Elements and Hypocrisy:**

Inside ideological groups, there is a gamble of hypocrisy in the determination of ladies contender for held seats. Hypocrisy happens when ladies are incorporated just to meet a share, without certified obligation to their strengthening and dynamic support in dynamic cycles. This sabotages the soul of orientation comprehensive administration.

To battle posturing, there is a requirement for inner party changes that focus on the consideration of ladies in positions of authority past held electorates. Ideological groups should cultivate a culture that qualities and advances the commitments of ladies pioneers, empowering their support in different party exercises and dynamic gatherings.

7. **Diversity and Inclusivity:**

Multifacetedness, the interconnected idea of social arrangements like race, class, and orientation, presents difficulties in the execution of reservations that are comprehensive of different personalities. Ladies from underestimated networks might confront intensified hindrances, including separation in light of both orientation and position or identity.

Tending to interconnection requires a thorough methodology that recognizes and effectively attempts to dispense with segregation on various fronts. Strategies and projects should be intended to be comprehensive and consider the special difficulties looked by ladies from different foundations. Backing gatherings and common society assume a critical part in guaranteeing that the execution of reservations is multifaceted and advances the interests, everything being equal.

8. **Restricted Execution in Higher Echelons:**

While reservations have been executed at the neighborhood and state levels, their expansion to higher echelons, like the public level, stays a test. Ladies' portrayal in India's Parliament and other focal establishments is still excessively low, restricting the effect of reservations on public policymaking.

Advocates for orientation comprehensive administration underline the requirement for stretching out reservations to higher echelons, guaranteeing that ladies' voices are heard at all degrees of direction. This requires a coordinated work to change existing regulations and gather political will to address the verifiable underrepresentation of ladies in focal foundations.

9. **Advancing Political Culture:**

The political culture in India, molded by verifiable practices and dug in power elements, presents a test to the compelling execution of bookings for ladies. Developing this political culture to embrace variety, inclusivity, and orientation balance requires a change in mentalities and practices that have been imbued over many years.

Drives advancing a more comprehensive political culture include instructive projects, public talk, and mindfulness crusades that challenge imbued inclinations. Empowering a more youthful age of pioneers who focus on variety and inclusivity is viewed as a critical technique to drive social change inside the political scene.

10. **Media Portrayal and Public Insight:**
Media portrayal assumes a pivotal part in molding public discernment, and ladies pioneers from saved bodies electorate frequently face difficulties connected with one-sided media inclusion. Generalizations and orientation predispositions propagated by the media can impact popular assessment and add to the propagation of customary orientation jobs.

11. **Legitimate Difficulties and Ambiguities:**

Legitimate difficulties and ambiguities in the execution of reservations, including understandings of existing regulations and possible escape clauses, present snags to successful execution. Clearness and consistency in lawful systems are fundamental to guarantee that reservations accomplish their planned objectives without potentially negative results.

7.1 Addressing reservations' limitations

While bookings for ladies in India have without a doubt been a urgent step towards accomplishing orientation equity in legislative issues, it is basic to recognize and address the limits intrinsic in this governmental policy regarding minorities in society strategy.

Perceiving these limits is fundamental for refining and growing the effect of reservations, guaranteeing that they contribute successfully to the bigger objective of making a more comprehensive and delegate political scene. In this investigation, we dig into the different impediments related with bookings for ladies and examine likely methodologies for tending to these difficulties.

1. **Emblematic Portrayal versus Meaningful Strengthening:**
One of the reactions coordinated at bookings for ladies is the differentiation between emblematic portrayal and considerable strengthening. While reservations might guarantee a mathematical presence of ladies in political bodies, it doesn't necessarily mean significant cooperation or impact. Ladies possessing saved seats might confront difficulties in applying significant impact inside the dynamic cycles, restricting the arrangement effect of their portrayal.
Tending to this restriction requires an extensive methodology. Past distributing saved seats, endeavors ought to zero in on giving preparation, mentorship, and administration improvement projects to upgrade the limit of ladies pioneers. Enabling ladies to effectively participate in strategy definition and support guarantees that their portrayal isn't simply emblematic however brings about meaningful commitments to administration.

2. **Interconnection and Inclusivity Difficulties:**
Reservations, while a basic step, may not adequately address the interconnected difficulties looked by ladies from underestimated networks. Ladies having a place with underestimated positions, clans, or strict minorities might experience intensified obstructions that reservations alone may not completely survived. The arrangement could incidentally sustain existing ordered progressions inside the ladies' portrayal structure.

To address this, a more nuanced approach is essential. Interconnection ought to be at the very front of policymaking, perceiving the exceptional difficulties looked by ladies with numerous personalities. Governmental policy regarding minorities in society systems should be intended to be comprehensive, taking into account the different foundations and encounters of ladies. This includes drawing in with networks, grasping their particular requirements, and creating arrangements that truly elevate all ladies.

3. **Restricted Effect at Higher Echelons:**
Reservations have fundamentally been executed at the neighborhood and state levels, and their effect on higher echelons of administration, for example, the public parliament, has been restricted. The convergence of ladies' portrayal at lower levels may not successfully convert into strategy changes at the more extensive public level, impeding the possible extraordinary effect of orientation comprehensive administration.

Techniques to address this limit include pushing for the expansion of reservations to higher echelons of administration. This requires a deliberate work to correct existing regulations, gather political will, and challenge the verifiable underrepresentation of ladies in focal establishments. By guaranteeing ladies' voices are heard at all levels, reservations can offer all the more essentially to molding public strategies.

4. **Insufficient Spotlight on Post-Reservation Backing:**
Reservations frequently need adequate post-execution support instruments for ladies pioneers. Once chose, ladies agents might confront segregation, restricted assets, and lacking help to release their obligations successfully. The shortfall of progressing support hampers their capacity to explore complex political scenes and achieve supported change.

Tending to this constraint includes making far reaching support structures for ladies pioneers. This incorporates mentorship programs, admittance to preparing and expertise improvement, and systems administration potential open doors. By cultivating a steady climate post-reservation, ladies pioneers can be better prepared to defeat difficulties and contribute definitively to administration.

5. **Ideological groups' Restricted Responsibility:**
Ideological groups, in certain occasions, display restricted obligation to the standards of orientation variety. Reservations might be seen as a consistence measure instead of a veritable obligation to cultivating comprehensive administration.

Gatherings might focus on handling ladies up-and-comers in saved seats without effectively advancing their administration improvement or more extensive support in party exercises.

To beat this, there is a requirement for inside party changes. Gatherings ought to effectively support and advance ladies' investment past held voting public. This includes making administration pipelines for ladies inside ideological groups, guaranteeing that they have amazing chances to participate in different party jobs and add to dynamic cycles.

6. **Dangers of Hypocrisy:**

The gamble of hypocrisy, where ladies are incorporated only to meet a share without veritable strengthening, is one more impediment of reservations. Token portrayal may not prompt significant commitments, and ladies possessing held seats could confront difficulties in acquiring validity and affecting strategy choices.

Systems to moderate hypocrisy include cultivating a culture inside ideological groups that esteems the certified consideration and strengthening of ladies. Inward party components ought to effectively empower ladies' support in dynamic cycles, furnishing them with chances to lead and contribute meaningfully to the party's objectives.

7. **Obstruction and Backfire:**

The execution of reservations can confront obstruction and reaction from different quarters, including people who see it as a danger to the current power elements. Social, cultural, and political opposition might appear in different structures, testing the smooth execution and acknowledgment of reservations.

To address obstruction, mindfulness missions and local area commitment drives are critical. Featuring the advantages of orientation comprehensive administration, dispersing fantasies, and cultivating open exchanges add to building acknowledgment. Coordinated effort with common society associations, backing gatherings, and assessment pioneers establishes a climate helpful for the fruitful execution of reservations.

8. **Intricacy in Execution:**

The intricacy in carrying out reservations, including strategic difficulties, managerial obstacles, and the requirement for lawful corrections, represents an impediment. The complexities engaged with guaranteeing the fair distribution of saved situates and keeping a harmony among variety and effectiveness can dismay.

Smoothing out the execution cycle requires a cooperative exertion between government bodies, political race commissions, and common society associations. Ordinary assessments and appraisals can assist with recognizing bottlenecks and regions for development. By working on systems and tending to calculated difficulties, the execution of reservations can turn out to be more successful.

9. **Potentially negative side-effects and Generalizing:**
   Reservations, while tending to orientation variations, may accidentally support generalizations about ladies' abilities. The discernment that ladies can prevail in governmental issues through reservations might add to generalizing and subvert the acknowledgment of their singular accomplishments and capabilities.
   To counter potentially negative results and generalizations, accentuation ought to be put on exhibiting the different accomplishments of ladies pioneers. Featuring examples of overcoming adversity that go past the saved seats helps challenge assumptions and advances a story that recognizes the skill of ladies in different influential positions.

10. **Restricted Spotlight on Neighborhood Administration:**

Reservations, while common in nearby administration, might not stand out in higher policymaking bodies. The effect of reservations on nearby administration might be eclipsed by the restricted spotlight on their expansion to higher echelons.

7.2 Ensuring effective implementation

Guaranteeing the powerful execution of bookings for ladies in India is a complex test that requires an exhaustive and supported exertion from policymakers, common society, and the more extensive local area. While reservations have been instrumental in tending to orientation variations in political portrayal, their prosperity relies on different variables going from legitimate systems to cultural mentalities. In this investigation, we dive into key viewpoints urgent for guaranteeing the successful execution of bookings for ladies.

1. **Lawful Changes and Reinforcing Systems:**
   A basic step towards successful execution is ceaseless legitimate change and the reinforcing of existing structures. Standard audits of regulation connected with reservations ought to be led to address any ambiguities, adjust to changing cultural requirements, and guarantee that the legitimate climate stays helpful for the objectives of orientation comprehensive administration.
   Legitimate changes shouldn't just zero in on the execution of reservations yet additionally address related issues, for example, avoidance of orientation based brutality, provocation, and oppression ladies in governmental issues. Reinforcing lawful systems makes a strong starting point for the fruitful execution of reservations and gives a premise to considering responsible the people who try to sabotage orientation uniformity in legislative issues.

2. **Limit Building and Authority Improvement:**
   Viable execution goes past the simple distribution of saved seats; it requires putting resources into the limit building and initiative improvement of ladies up-and-comers. Preparing projects, studios, and mentorship drives ought to be intended to outfit ladies with the fundamental abilities, information, and

certainty to explore the intricacies of political initiative.

Initiative improvement ought to stretch out past political race cycles to incorporate ceaseless help all through the residency of ladies delegates. By supporting a unit of able and enabled ladies pioneers, the effect of reservations isn't just maintained yet in addition enhanced as these pioneers contribute meaningfully to strategy plan and administration.

3. **Public Mindfulness Missions:**

Public discernment assumes a crucial part in the progress of bookings for ladies. Executing compelling public mindfulness crusades is fundamental to scatter legends, challenge generalizations, and assemble support for orientation comprehensive administration. These missions ought to feature the advantages of different portrayal, grandstand examples of overcoming adversity of ladies pioneers, and stress the positive effect of reservations on local area advancement.

Cooperative endeavors including government offices, common society associations, and news sources are basic for the progress of public mindfulness crusades. By cultivating a culture that qualities and supports ladies in authority, reservations can gather more extensive acknowledgment and add to the standardization of orientation variety in legislative issues.

4. **Local area Commitment and Grassroots Contribution:**

The outcome of reservations depends on the dynamic contribution and backing of neighborhood networks. Local area commitment drives ought to include exchange, conferences, and coordinated efforts with neighborhood pioneers and partners. It is vital to comprehend the one of a kind requirements and difficulties of various networks, guaranteeing that reservations are custom-made to address explicit settings.

Grassroots inclusion cultivates local area responsibility for strategy as well as establishes a favorable climate for ladies pioneers to interface with constituents. By building trust and tending to local area explicit worries, reservations become an impetus for positive change at the nearby level.

5. **Guaranteeing Satisfactory Assets:**

Satisfactory asset assignment is essential for the successful working of ladies delegates in held voting demographics. Guaranteeing that ladies approach monetary assets, regulatory help, and framework is fundamental for them to really do their obligations. This includes returning to monetary portions, making reserves explicitly reserved for ladies delegates, and carrying out systems to forestall the redirection of assets from held voting public.

Monetary and strategic help is especially critical for ladies up-and-comers during political races. By tending to asset inconsistencies, reservations can add to a more level battleground, empowering ladies to contend really and genuinely honorable serve their constituents.

6. **Measures to Battle Kickback and Obstruction:**

Reservations frequently face kickback and opposition from different quarters.

Executing measures to battle such provokes includes creating procedures to counter resistance and address misguided judgments. Political elements, common society associations, and backing bunches need to team up in creating accounts that underscore the positive commitments of ladies pioneers and the significance of orientation variety in administration.

Drawing in with doubters through open discoursed, scattering legends, and exhibiting the triumphs of ladies agents can assist with alleviating opposition. Making stages for useful conversations and including assessment pioneers in the process can add to building more extensive help for reservations.

7. **Standardizing Orientation Responsive Approaches:**

The progress of reservations is interwoven with the systematization of orientation responsive approaches across different areas. Past political portrayal, arrangements that address orientation differences in schooling, medical services, and work add to establishing a climate where ladies can flourish and effectively take part in open life.

Incorporating an orientation point of view into policymaking guarantees that the requirements and worries of ladies are deliberately thought of. This includes teaming up with government bodies, foundations, and common society associations to standard orientation responsive methodologies across various areas.

8. **Standard Checking and Assessment:**

Laying out systems for ordinary observing and assessment is fundamental for surveying the effect and adequacy of reservations. Progressing assessments ought to check the presentation of ladies agents, the degree of local area fulfillment, and the general commitment of reservations to administration. Input circles and information driven appraisals illuminate policymakers about regions that require improvement and guide future intercessions.

Common society associations, research foundations, and government bodies ought to team up in directing thorough assessments that go past mathematical portrayal to catch the subjective parts of ladies' support in legislative issues.

9. **Expansion of Reservations to Higher Echelons:**

While reservations have taken critical steps at the nearby and state levels, extending them to higher echelons, like the public parliament, stays a significant stage. Supporting for and executing reservations in higher regulative bodies guarantees that ladies' voices are heard at all degrees of navigation, adding to a more impartial and delegate political framework.

Political will, public help, and vital support endeavors are fundamental for the fruitful expansion of reservations to higher echelons. This requires a purposeful work to change existing regulations, challenge verifiable standards, and focus on the consideration of ladies in focal foundations.

10. **Worldwide Cooperation and Gaining from Worldwide Practices:**

Worldwide coordinated effort and gaining from worldwide prescribed procedures can give significant experiences to upgrading the execution of reservations. Teaming up with global associations, partaking in information sharing gatherings, and concentrating on effective models from different nations add to a more nuanced comprehension of orientation comprehensive administration.

7.3 Evaluating and refining policies based on feedback

The assessment and refinement of strategies, especially those connected with bookings for ladies in India, are essential parts of a responsive and dynamic administration framework. Ceaseless evaluation permits policymakers to check the effect of these approaches, recognize regions for development, and adjust techniques to address arising difficulties. In this investigation, we dive into the significance of assessing and refining approaches in view of criticism, analyzing how this iterative cycle adds to the viability and importance of bookings for ladies.

1. **Significance of Persistent Assessment:**

   Persistent assessment is a foundation of compelling policymaking, guaranteeing that strategies stay lined up with developing cultural necessities and desires. For bookings for ladies, standard appraisals give experiences into the exhibition of ladies delegates, the effect on neighborhood administration, and the general commitment to orientation comprehensive administration. As opposed to survey assessment as a one-time work out, a continuous interaction takes into consideration nuanced changes and responsive administration.

   Assessments ought to envelop both quantitative and subjective information, taking into account factors, for example, the quantity of ladies chose, their viability in navigation, and the impression of constituents towards orientation comprehensive administration. Ceaseless assessment frames the reason for proof based policymaking, cultivating a climate where approaches are custom-made to accomplish their planned goals.

2. **Input Components and Partner Commitment:**

   Hearty input systems are fundamental for acquiring assorted viewpoints and bits of knowledge into the working of reservations. Partner commitment, incorporating collaborations with ladies delegates, local area individuals, and common society associations, works with an extensive comprehension of the strategy's effect. Making stages for open discourse supports the dynamic co-operation of partners, cultivating straightforwardness and responsibility in the assessment cycle.

   Criticism components ought to be intended to catch the encounters, difficulties, and triumphs of ladies pioneers in held electorates. Reviews, municipal events, and counsels with different networks add to a rich wellspring of input, permitting policymakers to gather significant bits of knowledge and points of view.

3. **Subjective Evaluation of Ladies' Strengthening:**

   Past mathematical portrayal, the subjective evaluation of ladies' strengthening is vital for grasping the extraordinary effect of reservations.

Assessments ought to dive into whether ladies agents have had the option to practice office, contribute genuinely to strategy plan, and champion issues pertinent to their bodies electorate. Subjective evaluations catch the subtleties of strengthening, featuring the multi-layered parts of ladies' support in legislative issues.

Signs of subjective evaluation might remember ladies' administration for local area improvement projects, their effect on dynamic cycles, and their capacity to challenge customary standards. By underscoring subjective aspects, policymakers gain an all encompassing comprehension of how reservations add to the more extensive strengthening of ladies in the political circle.

4. **Tending to Difficulties and Bottlenecks:**

Assessment fills in as a demonstrative device to distinguish difficulties and bottlenecks that might hinder the successful execution of reservations. Whether it's asset incongruities, social obstruction, or regulatory obstacles, the assessment cycle assists pinpoint explicit regions that with requiring consideration. By tending to these difficulties, policymakers can refine the strategy system, guaranteeing that reservations are executed as well as capability ideally.

Systems for tending to difficulties might include designated intercessions, alterations to existing regulations, or local area explicit drives. The bits of knowledge acquired from assessments guide policymakers in creating custom fitted arrangements, cultivating a more responsive and versatile administration structure.

5. **Estimating Financial Effect:**

Assessing bookings for ladies ought to reach out past political measurements to incorporate the financial effect on networks. Surveying whether reservations add to the general improvement of saved bodies electorate, especially regarding schooling, medical care, and financial open doors, gives an extensive image of the strategy's impact.

Pointers for estimating financial effect might remember enhancements for proficiency rates, medical services availability, and monetary markers in saved supporters. The assessment cycle permits policymakers to comprehend the more extensive ramifications of reservations, guaranteeing that they contribute not exclusively to political portrayal yet in addition to the all encompassing improvement of networks.

6. **Consolidating Adaptability in Approach Plan:**

Assessment results frequently require changes and refinements to strategy plan. Policymakers ought to consolidate adaptability in the arrangement structure to oblige developing requirements and illustrations gained from assessments. This versatility guarantees that reservations stay receptive to evolving elements, empowering policymakers to adjust systems in light of exact proof and criticism.

Adaptability might include occasional audits of lawful structures, changes to strategy rules, or the acquaintance of beneficial measures with upgrade the viability of reservations. By embracing an adaptable methodology, policymakers exhibit a pledge to consistent improvement and an eagerness to answer the developing scene of administration.

7. **Advancing Inclusivity in Navigation:**

Assessments shed light on the inclusivity of dynamic cycles inside held voting public. Policymakers ought to survey whether ladies delegates effectively partake in key dynamic gatherings, add to strategy conversations, and are offered equivalent chances to shape the administration plan. Comprehensive direction heads past numeric portrayal to guarantee that ladies chiefs play a considerable part in forming strategies that influence their networks.

Assuming assessments uncover abberations in inclusivity, policymakers can acquaint measures with advance equivalent support. This might include preparing programs, mindfulness missions, and drives to challenge orientation inclinations inside dynamic bodies.

8. **Gaining from Worldwide Prescribed procedures:**

Assessments give an amazing chance to gain from worldwide prescribed procedures and encounters connected with orientation comprehensive administration. Relative examinations with different nations that have executed comparable governmental policy regarding minorities in society estimates offer significant bits of knowledge into what works and what can be moved along. Working together with worldwide associations and taking part in information sharing discussions enhances the policymaking system by drawing on a different scope of encounters.

Policymakers can use illustrations advanced worldwide to refine the plan and execution of reservations, guaranteeing that India benefits from an aggregate comprehension of successful methodologies for orientation comprehensive administration.

9. **Vital Correspondence and Account Building:**

The assessment interaction presents a chance for vital correspondence and story building. Positive results and examples of overcoming adversity coming about because of reservations ought to be really conveyed to general society, encouraging a story that features the advantages of orientation comprehensive administration. Vital correspondence helps counter bad insights, construct public help, and establish a positive climate for the supported execution of reservations.

Policymakers, as a team with correspondence specialists and common society associations, ought to create stories that commend the accomplishments of ladies pioneers and grandstand the positive effect of reservations on nearby turn of events.

10. **Iterative Arrangement Refinement:**

In view of assessment results and criticism, policymakers ought to take part in an iterative course of strategy refinement. This includes returning to strategy rules, making essential corrections, and adjusting methodologies to address arising difficulties. An iterative methodology highlights the powerful idea of administration and the obligation to persistent improvement.

Chapter 8

The Ripple Effect on Society

The execution of bookings for ladies in India has expansive ramifications that stretch out past the political domain, making a far reaching influence that impacts cultural mentalities, standards, and designs. This groundbreaking strategy, pointed toward tending to verifiable orientation variations, can possibly reshape the political scene as well as the more extensive social texture. In this investigation, we dive into the multi-layered expanding influence of ladies' reservations on Indian culture.

1. **Changing Orientation Standards and Discernments:**
   One of the essential far reaching influences of ladies' reservations is the progressive change of profoundly instilled orientation standards and discernments. By seeing ladies take on positions of authority in legislative issues, networks start to move customary generalizations that restricted ladies to explicit jobs. The perceivability of ladies in, influential places turns into a strong impetus for re-classifying cultural assumptions, empowering the acknowledgment of ladies as able pioneers.

   This change in discernment isn't bound to the political field yet pervades different parts of society. As ladies pioneers exhibit skill and viability, the story around ladies' capacities develops, encouraging a more comprehensive and moderate mentality.

2. **Strengthening Past Governmental issues:**
   While reservations explicitly target political portrayal, their effect reaches out to enable ladies in different circles of life. Ladies who expect positions of authority in legislative issues become images of strengthening, moving others to seek after schooling, vocations, and local area commitment. The strengthening catalyzed by reservations rises above the limits of legislative issues, impacting a more extensive range of chances for ladies in training, work, and decision-production inside families.

   The gradually expanding influence is especially articulated at the grassroots level, where ladies pioneers, supported by reservations, effectively take part in local area improvement projects, medical services drives, and instructive projects. The strengthening produced by political portrayal turns into a main thrust for positive change in the existences of ladies at large.

3. **Instructive Headway and Desires:**

The perceivability of ladies in governmental issues, politeness of reservations, fills in as a strong inspiration for instructive progression among little kids. As people group observer ladies pioneers settling on informed choices and adding to strategy detailing, yearnings among little kids are raised. The conviction that initiative isn't bound by orientation turns into a strong power in empowering young ladies to seek after training fully intent on taking on influential positions from now on.

The gradually expanding influence on instruction stretches out past individual goals to local area level changes. Reservations add to separating hindrances that prevent young ladies' admittance to schooling, encouraging a culture that qualities and puts resources into the instructive improvement, everything being equal, independent of orientation.

4. **Challenge to Man centric Designs:**

Ladies' reservations in legislative issues address an immediate test to male centric designs that have generally overwhelmed dynamic cycles. As ladies accept influential positions, they explore and upset laid out power elements, testing the customary authority of male administration. This test to male centric designs reaches out past legislative issues, impacting impression of power, capability, and authenticity inside cultural ordered progressions.

The actual demonstration of ladies possessing held seats in regulative bodies turns into a noticeable sign of the destroying of orientation based power lopsided characteristics. This not just makes space for different voices in administration yet in addition starts a trend for testing male centric standards across different circles of society.

5. **Local area Improvement and Comprehensive Strategies:**

Ladies pioneers, upheld by reservations, frequently focus on local area improvement drives and promoter for arrangements that address the requirements of underestimated gatherings.

The expanding influence of these endeavors is felt as additional comprehensive and evenhanded strategies that think about the different necessities of networks. Reservations add to a change in strategy needs, underlining civil rights, medical services access, and monetary open doors for all, consequently encouraging a more comprehensive and responsive administration structure.

The attention on local area advancement rises above political limits, impacting cultural mentalities towards aggregate prosperity. The accentuation on inclusivity and fair asset distribution turns into a core value in governmental issues as well as in local area drove drives.

6. **Job Demonstrating and Mentorship:**
   Ladies pioneers rising up out of reservations become strong good examples for people in the future of ladies. Their processes move different ladies yearn for positions of authority and participate in open life. Furthermore, ladies pioneers frequently participate in mentorship programs, effectively supporting and directing hopeful ladies pioneers. This mentorship dynamic makes a positive criticism circle, sustaining a culture of help and cooperation among ladies.
   The far reaching influence of job demonstrating and mentorship stretches out to the working environment, instructive establishments, and local area associations. Ladies who have seen the effect of reservations are bound to look for and give mentorship, adding to the development of a steady environment for ladies' progression.

7. **Decrease in Orientation Based Savagery:**
   The expanded perceivability and impact of ladies in governmental issues, worked with by reservations, add to a decrease in orientation based savagery. As ladies gain noticeable quality in dynamic cycles, cultural perspectives towards savagery and oppression ladies go through a change. The declaration of ladies' privileges inside political circles significantly affects cultural standards, establishing a climate less open minded toward orientation based brutality.
   Reservations subsequently become an essential device in the more extensive work to challenge and destroy profoundly imbued structures that sustain brutality against ladies. The far reaching influence on diminishing orientation based savagery highlights the capability of reservations to add to a more secure and more evenhanded society.

8. **Upgraded Political Cooperation of Ladies:**
   The effect of ladies' reservations reaches out past the seats straightforwardly impacted by the approach. Ladies who witness the achievement and effect of saved seats are bound to take part in political support at different levels. The expanding influence is obvious in expanded ladies' portrayal in nearby administration, local area associations, and grassroots developments. The standardization of ladies' support in political cycles turns into an impetus for a more extensive and more supported contribution in molding the political scene.
   As ladies become dynamic supporters of political talk, the variety of points of view inside political dynamic bodies widens, prompting more complete and nuanced strategy results.

9. **Social Shift Towards Orientation Equity:**
   Bookings for ladies add to a social shift towards orientation equity, testing well established standards and practices that sustain orientation based segregation. The actual presence of reservations challenges cultural discernments about ladies' jobs and capacities. After some time, this social shift impacts the assumptions put on ladies and the open doors made accessible to them inside families, networks, and work environments.

The social change cultivated by reservations lays the basis for a general public that values orientation correspondence as a major guideline, perceiving the intrinsic worth and capability of each and every individual independent of orientation.

10. **Advancement of Comprehensive Administration Values:**

The far reaching influence of ladies' reservations finishes in the advancement of comprehensive administration values. The strategy turns into an impetus for implanting standards of inclusivity, variety, and portrayal inside the texture of administration. The perceivability of ladies pioneers in legislative issues converts into a more extensive obligation to mirroring the different necessities and desires of the whole populace.

8.1 Changing societal attitudes towards women in leadership

The scene of cultural mentalities towards ladies in positions of authority has gone through a significant change in ongoing many years, mirroring a shift towards perceiving and embracing the capability, potential, and authenticity of ladies as successful pioneers. This development in cultural discernments is molded by a juncture of elements, including changing social standards, expanded instructive open doors for ladies, and the noticeable presence of ladies in administrative roles across different areas. In this investigation, we dig into the elements of this cultural shift, looking at the critical impetuses and the ramifications for cultivating a more comprehensive and impartial society.

1. **Instructive Strengthening:**
   A critical impetus for changing cultural perspectives towards ladies in initiative is the rising accentuation on instructive strengthening. As additional ladies access and succeed in instructive foundations, there is a relating shift in cultural view of ladies' scholarly capacities and reasonableness for influential positions. Schooling fills in as a vehicle for destroying conventional generalizations and testing orientation based presumptions, preparing for a more edified and comprehensive comprehension of ladies' possible in administration.
   The groundbreaking effect of instruction reaches out past individual strengthening to impacting aggregate perspectives. Social orders that focus on and put resources into ladies' schooling will generally be more open to ladies expecting positions of authority, perceiving the worth of assorted viewpoints in dynamic cycles.

2. **Perceivability of Ladies in Different Positions of authority:**
   The perceivability of ladies in different influential positions across areas plays had a pivotal impact in reshaping cultural perspectives. Ladies pioneers in governmental issues, business, the scholarly world, and different fields act as good examples, testing assumptions about the restricted jobs ladies can play. As ladies show skill and viability in administrative roles, cultural discernments develop to

embrace a more comprehensive meaning of initiative.

The perceivability of ladies pioneers additionally counters generalizations and predispositions by displaying the assorted manners by which ladies can succeed in authority. This perceivability fills in as a strong counter-story, impacting mentalities towards individual ladies pioneers as well as towards the more extensive acknowledgment of ladies in administration across various spaces.

3. **Changing Social Stories:**
   Social stories assume a huge part in molding cultural perspectives, and there has been a recognizable change in social stories that depict ladies in initiative. Media, writing, and mainstream society progressively include stories that feature ladies' administration characteristics, flexibility, and accomplishments. These stories challenge age-old models that restricted ladies to uninvolved or optional jobs, adding to a reconsidering of ladies' parts in the public eye.

   Socially important depictions of ladies in initiative, whether in films, books, or media inclusion, give an offset to verifiable generalizations. By exhibiting ladies as fit pioneers, these social stories add to normalizing the possibility of ladies in influential positions, encouraging acknowledgment and lessening protection from ladies accepting, influential places.

4. **Headways in Orientation Correspondence Support:**
   The coordinated endeavors of orientation correspondence supporters and developments have essentially affected cultural mentalities towards ladies in authority. Backing drives feature the significance of orientation variety, challenge unfair practices, and call for equivalent open doors for ladies in administrative roles. The preparation of public talk around these issues makes mindfulness, supports discourse, and cultivates an aggregate obligation to destroying hindrances that obstruct ladies' advancement in positions of authority.

   Orientation balance promotion significantly affects cultural perspectives by testing imbued predispositions and encouraging a feeling of aggregate liability regarding making a more comprehensive and impartial society.

   The reverberation of these backing endeavors is clear in strategy changes, corporate drives, and cultural assumptions that undeniably focus on orientation equity in administration.

5. **Acknowledgment of Ladies' Authority Skills:**
   A fundamental part of changing cultural mentalities towards ladies in administration is the developing acknowledgment of ladies' authority capabilities. As associations and organizations focus on meritocracy over orientation based contemplations, ladies have more open doors to exhibit their abilities, gifts, and authority keenness. This change in acknowledgment challenges the thought that administration is intrinsically attached to orientation and highlights that successful authority is dependent upon ability and legitimacy.

   The affirmation of ladies' administration capabilities isn't just fundamental for individual headway yet additionally adds to more extensive cultural discernments. It builds up the comprehension that different administration groups, containing all kinds of people, are bound to cultivate development, imagination, and extensive navigation.

6. **Institutional Changes Supporting Orientation Inclusivity:**

The reception of institutional strategies and practices that advance orientation inclusivity is a basic empowering influence of changing cultural mentalities towards ladies in initiative. Associations that execute measures, for example, sexually unbiased enlistment processes, mentorship programs for ladies, and family-accommodating strategies signal a pledge to establishing a comprehensive workplace. These institutional changes enable ladies inside unambiguous associations as well as add to reshaping more extensive cultural assumptions.

As additional organizations take on comprehensive practices, they set a trend that impacts cultural standards. The standardization of orientation comprehensive strategies sends a strong message about the similarity of ladies with positions of authority, testing generalizations and predispositions that might persevere in different areas.

7. **Consolation of Administration Goals from Adolescence:**

Changing cultural perspectives towards ladies in administration frequently starts with the consolation of administration yearnings since early on. Families, teachers, and networks assume a urgent part in cultivating a climate where young ladies are urged to imagine themselves as pioneers. Instructive educational plans that feature the accomplishments of ladies pioneers, mentorship programs, and extracurricular exercises that support initiative abilities add to making a pipeline of certain and hopeful ladies pioneers.

The support of initiative yearnings from youth upsets conventional orientation standards, imparting the conviction that administration is a reasonable and positive way for people paying little heed to orientation. This early consolation establishes the groundwork for a more comprehensive and strong society.

8. **Systems administration and Mentorship Open doors:**

Systems administration and mentorship open doors assume a vital part in forming ladies' directions in administration. The foundation of expert organizations, mentorship projects, and discussions for information trade makes a steady environment that enables ladies in their authority processes. Admittance to mentorship and organizations upgrades individual authority abilities as well as works with the sharing of encounters and experiences that challenge cultural generalizations.

The effect of systems administration and mentorship reaches out past individual examples of overcoming adversity to impact cultural discernments. As additional ladies benefit from these amazing open doors and climb to administrative roles, the story around ladies' skill and reasonableness for positions of authority picks up speed.

9. **Lawful Systems Advancing Orientation Fairness:**
   Lawful systems that advance orientation fairness and restrict separation in view of orientation contribute essentially to changing cultural mentalities towards ladies in administration. Against segregation regulations, arrangements advancing equivalent compensation, and measures to address working environment provocation establish a climate where ladies can try to and achieve administrative roles unafraid of fundamental inclinations or separation.
   Lawful systems act as a useful asset for destroying institutional hindrances and testing cultural standards that propagate orientation based separation. As these lawful systems gain noticeable quality, they add to a more extensive social shift towards perceiving and esteeming ladies' commitments in administration.

10. **Effect of Worldwide Developments for Orientation Fairness:**

Worldwide developments for orientation uniformity, like #MeToo and Ladies' Walks, significantly affect molding cultural perspectives towards ladies in administration. These developments cause to notice issues of orientation segregation, badgering, and disparity, cultivating a shared mindset about the significance of orientation inclusivity. The worldwide fortitude showed through these developments reverberates locally, impacting cultural perspectives and assumptions about the job of ladies in authority.

8.2 Impact on gender roles and stereotypes

The effect of changing cultural mentalities towards ladies in administration is complicatedly associated with the change of orientation jobs and generalizations. As ladies progressively expect noticeable situations in different positions of authority, there is a substantial gradually expanding influence on how society sees, characterizes, and doles out jobs in light of orientation. In this investigation, we dig into the significant effect on orientation jobs and generalizations catalyzed by the developing scene of ladies in authority.

1. **Re-imagined Ideas of Authority Ability:**
   The rising perceivability of ladies in administrative roles challenges conventional ideas of authority capability that have generally been formed by orientation predispositions. As ladies show their capacities in chief, political, and administrative jobs, cultural discernments advance to perceive that authority capabilities are not intrinsically orientation explicit. This redefinition of administration capability adds to destroying generalizations that have confined ladies to specific jobs considered more reasonable by conventional standards.
   The thought that powerful administration requires explicit orientation credits is supplanted by a comprehension that administration is a range of abilities established in characteristics like key reasoning, correspondence, and direction, credits that rise above orientation limits.

2. **Change in Parental and Guardian Jobs:**

The effect on orientation jobs reaches out to familial and parental figure elements. As ladies expect high-profile administrative roles, there is a continuous change in conventional assumptions about parental and providing care jobs. The story changes from characterizing ladies principally as guardians to recognizing their ability to offset requesting proficient jobs with family obligations. This shift difficulties profoundly instilled generalizations about the division of work inside families and opens roads for more fair circulation of providing care liabilities.

The developing orientation jobs in the family circle are reflected by a developing acknowledgment of men as dynamic supporters of providing care liabilities, encouraging a more adjusted and comprehensive way to deal with familial jobs.

3. **Challenge to Gendered Proficient Generalizations:**

The presence of ladies in authority challenges gendered proficient generalizations that have generally restricted ladies to explicit enterprises or jobs. As ladies succeed in areas generally overwhelmed by men, like innovation, money, and science, the impression of what is "suitable" or "satisfactory" vocation ways for ladies widens. This difficulties the cultural story that specific callings are innately male-overwhelmed and consigns ladies to a restricted arrangement of choices.

The breaking of gendered proficient generalizations extends vocation decisions for ladies as well as impacts more youthful ages, empowering them to seek after professions in view of their inclinations and aptitudes as opposed to adjusting to orientation standards.

4. **Strengthening of Ladies as Chiefs:**

The expanded portrayal of ladies in administrative roles enables them as chiefs, testing generalizations that question ladies' thinking skills. As ladies go with vital choices in meeting rooms, government workplaces, and associations, the story shifts from seeing ladies as hesitant or sincerely headed to recognizing their ability for sound and powerful navigation.

This strengthening reaches out to all parts of life, empowering ladies to effectively partake in decision-production inside families, networks, and individual circles. The developing view of ladies as proficient leaders adds to separating obstructions that have generally restricted ladies' organization.

5. **Destroying Generalizations about Desire:**

The apparent outcome of ladies in administration challenges generalizations about ladies' desire and vocation goals. Generalizations that depict aggressive ladies as forceful or decisive from a negative perspective are exposed as ladies rise to influential positions with certainty and assurance. This difficulties the story that aggressive ladies are exceptions and highlights the significance of perceiving and cultivating desire as a positive quality paying little mind to orientation.

The developing impression of ladies as aggressive pioneers adds to a social shift where ladies are urged to seek after their expert objectives without confronting cultural kickback or being exposed to gendered assumptions.

6. **Portrayal in Modern Fields:**

The effect on orientation jobs is particularly articulated in fields that were customarily viewed as modern for ladies. As ladies break into STEM (Science, Innovation, Designing, and Arithmetic) fields, enter the military, and seek after vocations in generally male-overwhelmed areas, generalizations about the impediments of ladies in unambiguous callings are destroyed. This development of portrayal challenges the imbued conviction that specific fields are intrinsically unacceptable or distant to ladies.

The perceivability of ladies prevailing in contemporary fields not just enables ladies to investigate different profession ways yet additionally empowers a more comprehensive way to deal with ability enlistment and improvement.

7. **Social Redefinition of Womanliness:**

The changing scene of ladies in influential positions adds to a social redefinition of womanliness that rises above conventional generalizations. The view of womanliness develops past barely characterized jobs and attributes, perceiving that ladies can encapsulate a different scope of characteristics, including strength, flexibility, and decisiveness. This redefinition challenges the double idea of gentility as frail or compliant, cultivating a more comprehensive comprehension of orientation character.

The social redefinition of gentility adds to separating cultural assumptions that limit ladies to adjusting to assumptions of how they ought to act, dress, or communicate their thoughts.

8. **Advancement of Balance between fun and serious activities for All Sexual orientations:**

As ladies in authority explore the sensitive harmony between proficient obligations and individual life, there is a distinguishable effect on orientation jobs connected with balance between fun and serious activities. The story shifts from outlining balance between fun and serious activities as an overwhelmingly ladies' issue to remembering it as a widespread concern material to all sexes. The affirmation that people, paying little heed to orientation, esteem a harmony among expert and individual life challenges generalizations that connection balance between fun and serious activities exclusively to ladies' providing care jobs.

The advancement of balance between serious and fun activities as a common need adds to more comprehensive work environment strategies and difficulties generalizations that sustain inconsistent assumptions for people in adjusting work and everyday life.

9. **Influence on Multifacetedness:**

The diversity of orientation with different parts of personality, like race, nationality, and financial foundation, is affected by the changing scene of ladies in authority. As ladies from different foundations expect administrative roles, there is a nuanced influence on the generalizations related with diversity. The story grows to perceive that initiative characteristics are not homogenous however converge with a heap of personalities and encounters.

This nuanced understanding difficulties cliché suspicions about how various gatherings of ladies explore and add to influential positions, encouraging a more comprehensive and multifaceted viewpoint.

10. **Effect on Media Depictions:**

The changing orientation jobs and generalizations are reflected in media depictions of ladies in administration. As ladies expect different influential positions, media stories shift from supporting conventional generalizations to introducing a more sensible and changed portrayal of ladies' capacities. Positive and nuanced media portrayals add to forming cultural insights and testing instilled generalizations propagated by authentic predispositions.

8.3 The role of education and awareness

The job of training and mindfulness in molding cultural perspectives, cultivating inclusivity, and testing generalizations is basic to the development of a moderate and evenhanded society. Training fills in as an incredible asset for illuminating people, advancing decisive reasoning, and developing a culture of understanding and acknowledgment. In this investigation, we dive into the multi-layered job of schooling and mindfulness in reshaping cultural points of view, testing generalizations, and establishing the groundwork for an additional comprehensive and illuminated future.

1. **Instructive Strengthening as an Impetus:**
   Training remains as a foundation in the change of cultural mentalities. It fills in as an impetus for enabling people with information, decisive reasoning abilities, and a more extensive perspective. As school systems focus on inclusivity and variety, people are presented to a rich embroidery of viewpoints that challenge generalizations and cultivate a more nuanced comprehension of different characters.

   Past the securing of scholarly information, schooling assumes a significant part in molding values, perspectives, and relational connections. An educational program that underlines fairness, regard, and variety outfits people with the instruments to address generalizations and add to the production of a more comprehensive society.

2. **Developing Decisive Reasoning and Insightful Abilities:**
   Instruction, when intended to develop decisive reasoning and scientific abilities, engages people to address generalizations and challenge winning inclinations. An educational program that urges understudies to dissect verifiable stories, dismantle media portrayals, and participate in open conversations about cultural standards cultivates a culture of scholarly interest and free thought.

Through the improvement of decisive reasoning abilities, people become more proficient at perceiving and destroying generalizations, laying the preparation for a general public that values variety and rejects oversimplified classifications in view of orientation, race, or different characters.

3. **Comprehensive Educational program and Portrayal:**
The substance and portrayal inside instructive materials and educational programs assume a critical part in forming cultural perspectives. A comprehensive educational program that mirrors the variety of human encounters, commitments, and points of view helps separate generalizations by introducing a more exact and exhaustive depiction of various gatherings.

At the point when people experience different voices, chronicles, and accomplishments inside their instructive excursion, they are better prepared to challenge assumptions and foster a more nuanced comprehension of the extravagance inborn in human variety. Portrayal in instructive materials turns into a mirror that mirrors the variety of the world and adds to the destroying of generalizations.

4. **Advancing Orientation Uniformity Instruction:**
Orientation uniformity training is a specific feature of instructive strengthening that assumes a focal part in testing generalizations connected with orientation jobs and assumptions. By incorporating orientation uniformity into educational plans, schooling systems add to destroying generalizations that propagate imbalance.

This incorporates testing thoughts of conventional orientation jobs, stressing the significance of assent and conscious connections, and featuring the accomplishments of ladies in different fields.

Orientation fairness schooling not just gives people the information to fundamentally evaluate generalizations yet additionally imparts a feeling of obligation to effectively add to making a more impartial society.

5. **Mindfulness Missions and Effort Projects:**
Past proper schooling, mindfulness missions and effort programs assume a urgent part in molding cultural perspectives. These drives frequently target explicit issues, testing generalizations and predispositions common in the public eye. Whether zeroed in on advancing LGBTQ+ privileges, testing racial generalizations, or supporting for handicap consideration, mindfulness crusades make spaces for discourse, reflection, and change.

By utilizing different stages like online entertainment, local area occasions, and instructive studios, mindfulness crusades add to destroying generalizations by introducing counter-stories, cultivating compassion, and welcoming people to scrutinize their own predispositions.

6. **Media Education as a Safeguard Against Generalizations:**
During a time where media assumes a focal part in molding public discernments, media proficiency turns into a basic part of training and mindfulness. People

need to foster the abilities to fundamentally survey media portrayals, perceive generalizations propagated by different types of media, and explore through the complicated scene of data.

Instructive projects that attention on media proficiency enable people to dismantle generalizations present in notices, movies, news, and virtual entertainment. This elevated mindfulness goes about as a safeguard against the support of destructive generalizations and energizes a seriously insightful commitment with media content.

7. **Various Good examples and Rousing Figures:**

Instruction and mindfulness add to the advancement of different good examples and moving figures who resist generalizations and challenge cultural assumptions. Finding out about people who have beaten boundaries, broke biased based impediments, and made critical commitments to different fields turns into a wellspring of motivation.

Openness to different good examples cultivates a feeling of probability and desire among people, empowering them to seek after their objectives independent of cultural generalizations. Praising the accomplishments of people from different foundations turns into a strong method for widening viewpoints and reshaping cultural stories.

8. **Local area Commitment and Exchange:**

Instruction and mindfulness are not restricted to formal instructive settings; local area commitment and open discourse are similarly essential. Local area based programs that empower conversations about generalizations, predispositions, and inclusivity make spaces for people to share their encounters, challenge misinterpretations, and by and large imagine a more fair future.

Exchanges inside networks, worked with through studios, discussions, or local area driven drives, cultivate grasping, sympathy, and a common obligation to destroying generalizations that sustain segregation and rejection.

9. **Worldwide Viewpoints and Intercultural Schooling:**

In an interconnected world, schooling that embraces worldwide viewpoints and intercultural understanding is fundamental. Presenting people to different societies, customs, and perspectives encourages a feeling of worldwide citizenship and difficulties generalizations established in ethnocentrism or xenophobia.

Intercultural training urges people to see the value in the wealth of human variety, testing generalizations by stressing the common mankind that rises above social, racial, or ethnic contrasts.

10. **Long lasting Advancing as a Persistent Test to Generalizations:**

Deep rooted learning, portrayed by a promise to persistent training and self-awareness, turns into a nonstop test to generalizations. As people participate in continuous growth opportunities, they stay open to groundbreaking thoughts, various viewpoints, and advancing cultural standards.

Chapter 9

Looking Ahead - Future Possibilities and Challenges

Looking forward, the direction of cultural mentalities towards ladies' strengthening in India, especially through reservation wins, holds both promising potential outcomes and diligent difficulties. The advancement of orientation elements is profoundly entwined with the socio-political scene, social movements, and continuous endeavors to destroy dug in disparities. In this investigation, we dive into the future prospects and difficulties that lie not too far off.

1. Arising Conceivable outcomes:

As India keeps on wrestling with the mind boggling embroidery of orientation elements, there are a few promising potential outcomes not too far off.

1. **Economic Strengthening:**
   The expanded portrayal of ladies in political circles, worked with by reservation wins, can possibly convert into more extensive financial strengthening. Ladies' dynamic cooperation in dynamic cycles can prompt strategies that address orientation explicit financial difficulties, encouraging a more comprehensive and evenhanded economy.
   Monetary strengthening isn't just about admittance to amazing open doors yet additionally includes tending to wage holes, advancing business among ladies, and guaranteeing fair work rehearses. Reservation wins can act as an impetus for establishing a climate where ladies are available in influential positions as well as effectively adding to molding monetary strategies that elevate ladies across all layers of society.

2. **Social Change:**
   The booking wins can possibly catalyze a more extensive social change. As ladies possess administrative roles, cultural perspectives towards orientation jobs and assumptions might go through a change in outlook. The perceivability of

ladies in persuasive jobs difficulties conventional generalizations and standards, making space for a more comprehensive comprehension of the different jobs ladies can play in the public eye.

This social change stretches out past metropolitan habitats to rustic networks, where the effect of such changes can be especially significant. The far reaching influence of ladies in administrative roles can rouse little kids, challenge orientation standards, and add to a more populist society.

3. Legislative Force:

The progress of bookings for ladies might possibly make regulative energy for additional changes. As ladies in administration exhibit their viability, there might be expanded political will to address other squeezing orientation related issues. This remembers changes for regions like medical care, instruction, and viciousness against ladies.

Regulative force can reach out to the requirement of existing regulations that safeguard ladies' freedoms and the making of new strategies that address arising difficulties. The victory of ladies' reservations can be a venturing stone towards a more exhaustive lawful structure that guarantees the prosperity and freedoms of ladies are focused on.

2. Proceeded with Difficulties:

In spite of the promising prospects, the excursion towards orientation uniformity in India faces diligent difficulties that require supported exertion and vital mediations.

1. **Intersectionality and Inclusivity:**
   One of the difficulties lies in tending to the diversity of orientation with different factors like standing, class, and religion. While bookings for ladies address a huge step in the right direction, the encounters of ladies from minimized networks might contrast essentially. Inclusivity inside the women's activist development is urgent to guaranteeing that the advantages of strengthening arrive at ladies across different foundations.

   Recognizing and tending to the multifacetedness of orientation based separation is fundamental for making approaches and drives that are really comprehensive and fair. Inability to do so chances sustaining variations among ladies and building up existing orders.

2. **Cultural and Social Obstruction:**
   Social and social protection from changes in conventional orientation jobs stays a considerable test. Profoundly imbued generalizations, male centric standards, and protection from shifts in power elements can hinder the advancement of orientation equity drives. Much of the time, ladies in administrative roles face obstruction both inside political circles and inside their networks.

   Beating social and social obstruction requires official measures as well as complete mindfulness crusades and instructive drives. Changing cultural mentalities requires an aggregate work to challenge well established convictions and advance a more comprehensive and tolerating society.

3. Violence Against Ladies:

In spite of headways, savagery against ladies keeps on being an unavoidable test. Ladies in administrative roles might confront elevated gambles, including badgering and dangers. Moreover, the more extensive test of tending to viciousness against ladies at all degrees of society stays a basic issue that requires coordinated endeavors.

Making a general public liberated from viciousness against ladies includes lawful measures as well as social moves that reject the standardization of such way of behaving. Engaging ladies in initiative to advocate for and implement regulations against orientation based savagery is a critical stage in tending to this unavoidable test.

3. Systems for What's in store:

Exploring the future prospects and difficulties requires key and complex methodologies that address the underlying drivers of orientation disparity.

1. **Holistic Schooling:**
   Putting resources into comprehensive training that goes past conventional scholarly subjects is fundamental. Complete instructive projects ought to remember parts for orientation uniformity, ladies' freedoms, and the commitments of ladies to different fields. Comprehensive training encourages decisive reasoning, challenges generalizations, and establishes the groundwork for a more comprehensive society.

2. **Intersectional Strategies:**
   Strategies pointed toward enabling ladies should be multifaceted, perceiving the novel difficulties looked by ladies from minimized networks. Interconnected strategies consider factors like position, class, and religion, guaranteeing that the advantages of strengthening arrive at all ladies, no matter what their social foundation.

3. **Community Commitment:**
   Local area commitment is critical to defeating social obstruction. Drives that include networks in conversations about orientation correspondence, the advantages of ladies' strengthening, and the results of sustaining generalizations can prompt more significant and enduring change.

4. **Legal Changes and Execution:**
   While administrative triumphs are critical, viable execution of existing regulations and the nonstop quest for lawful changes are similarly significant. Guaranteeing that regulations safeguarding ladies' privileges are upheld, and tending to holes in regulation, adds to making an all the more and fair society.

5. **Media Backing:**

Utilizing media as a device for promotion is essential. Positive and comprehensive media portrayals of ladies, as well as mindfulness crusades that challenge generalizations, assume a part in forming public discernments. Joint efforts between news sources, promotion gatherings, and instructive foundations can intensify these endeavors.

9.1 Potential improvements and expansions

Opening the maximum capacity of ladies' strengthening in India requires a coordinated exertion towards consistent improvement and development of existing drives. While critical steps have been made, there are regions that request thoughtfulness regarding make a more comprehensive, impartial, and engaging climate for ladies. In this investigation, we dive into likely upgrades and extensions across different spaces to improve the scene of ladies' strengthening in India.

1. **Financial Strengthening through Expertise Improvement:**

   To support monetary strengthening, there is a squeezing need for designated expertise improvement programs that take care of the different requirements of ladies. Outfitting ladies with important abilities improves their employability as well as engages them to investigate pioneering open doors. Professional preparation drives, mentorship projects, and admittance to assets can add to building a talented and engaged female labor force.

   Growing expertise improvement projects to envelop arising areas like innovation, reasonable horticulture, and environmentally friendly power guarantees that ladies are members as well as pioneers in forming India's financial future.

   Government and confidential area coordinated effort in making expertise improvement centers can furnish ladies with the devices expected to flourish in a quickly developing position market.

2. **Improved Admittance to Quality Instruction:**

   While steps have been made in working on young ladies' admittance to schooling, there is a requirement for supported endeavors to improve the nature of training. This includes putting resources into framework, instructor preparing, and educational plan improvement to establish a comprehensive instructive climate. Furthermore, advancing STEM (Science, Innovation, Designing, and Math) training for young ladies can make ready for expanded portrayal in fields customarily overwhelmed by men.

   The development of grant programs, particularly for young ladies from minimized networks, can separate monetary obstructions that upset instructive pursuits. Unique consideration ought to be given to tending to exit rates among young adult young ladies, guaranteeing that they progress flawlessly from essential to auxiliary and advanced education.

3. **Pioneering Environments for Ladies:**

   Cultivating innovative biological systems custom-made to the necessities of ladies is crucial for financial strengthening. This includes making encouraging groups of people, giving admittance to capital, and offering mentorship programs. Government drives, for example, Begin up India, need to consolidate orientation explicit contemplations to guarantee that ladies business visionaries get the essential help to flourish.

Growing drives that advance ladies drove ventures in areas like medical care, training, and innovation can contribute not exclusively to individual monetary strengthening yet additionally to more extensive cultural turn of events. Public-private organizations can assume a pivotal part in establishing an empowering climate for ladies to lay out and scale their organizations.

4. **Medical services Drives with an Orientation Focal point:**
   Wellbeing stays a basic part of ladies' strengthening, and there is a requirement for medical services drives with an orientation delicate methodology. Extending admittance to regenerative medical care administrations, maternal wellbeing projects, and mindfulness crusades on ladies' medical problems can add to generally prosperity. Specific medical care drives ought to address the remarkable wellbeing challenges looked by ladies, including feminine cleanliness, maternal mortality, and non-transmittable illnesses.

   Public mindfulness missions ought to endeavor to destigmatize ladies' wellbeing concerns and advance open discussions. Coordinating computerized wellbeing arrangements and telemedicine can likewise further develop admittance to medical care administrations, especially in remote and underserved regions.

5. **Legitimate Changes and Authorization:**
   While official systems exist to safeguard ladies' privileges, there is a requirement for nonstop lawful changes and powerful implementation. Fortifying regulations connected with orientation based brutality, work environment badgering, and property privileges can add to a more secure and more evenhanded society. Public mindfulness missions ought to instruct ladies about their freedoms and lawful response systems.

   Growing the span of legitimate guide benefits and making open complaint redressal systems can guarantee that ladies have the help they need to look for equity. Joint effort between the general set of laws, policing, and common society associations is fundamental to make a complete and successful structure for ladies' security.

6. **Political Cooperation and Portrayal:**
   While the presentation of reservations has expanded ladies' portrayal in nearby administration, there is opportunity to get better at more elevated levels of political authority. Extending the extent of reservations to incorporate higher regulative bodies, like state congregations and the public parliament, can additionally improve ladies' political investment.

   Ideological groups ought to effectively empower and advance ladies pioneers, guaranteeing that ladies have equivalent chances to challenge races and stand firm on authority situations. Public mindfulness missions can feature the significance of ladies' voices in political navigation and challenge generalizations that might obstruct their political aspirations.

7. **Mechanical Incorporation for Ladies:**
Crossing over the computerized orientation partition is fundamental for the strengthening of ladies in the advanced age. Drives that attention on computerized proficiency and innovation preparing for ladies can improve their support in the advanced economy. Growing admittance to reasonable cell phones and web availability can enable ladies with data, assets, and systems administration open doors.
Government and confidential area joint effort can prompt the production of innovation centers and hatcheries explicitly intended for ladies. This guarantees that ladies have what it takes and assets to use innovation for training, business venture, and systems administration.

8. **Family and Local area Commitment Projects:**
Building support structures inside families and networks is pivotal for ladies' strengthening. Programs that draw in families and networks in discussions about orientation uniformity, ladies' privileges, and the advantages of ladies' strengthening can add to moving social standards. Extending people group based drives that include men and young men in upholding for orientation equity encourages a more comprehensive methodology.
The production of public venues that give data, backing, and advising for ladies can act as places of refuge for discourse and strengthening. Social and creative drives can likewise be utilized to challenge generalizations and commend ladies' accomplishments.

9. **Media Proficiency and Orientation Delicate Substance:**
Advancing media proficiency and guaranteeing orientation touchy substance in media stages assume a pivotal part in molding cultural mentalities. Extending media proficiency programs in schools and networks can prepare people, particularly the adolescent, to fundamentally examine media portrayals and challenge generalizations. Joint effort between media associations and ladies' backing gatherings can prompt the formation of content that reflects assorted accounts and positive depictions of ladies.
Administrative structures ought to energize dependable and comprehensive media works on, encouraging a climate where media assumes a productive part in advancing orientation fairness.

10. **Worldwide Cooperation for Ladies' Strengthening:**

Perceiving that ladies' strengthening is a worldwide issue, there is a requirement for expanded coordinated effort on the global stage. Extending associations with worldwide associations, sharing prescribed procedures, and taking part in global gatherings zeroed in on ladies' freedoms can give significant experiences and backing. Drawing in with worldwide developments and missions enhances the effect of ladies' strengthening drives and makes an aggregate voice for change.

9.2 Policy recommendations

Making successful arrangement proposals is fundamental for propelling ladies' strengthening in India. A thorough arrangement of strategies should address the intricate and interconnected difficulties that block ladies' advancement across different spaces. In this investigation, we dig into strategy proposals that envelop monetary strengthening, training, medical care, lawful changes, political support, innovation, family and local area commitment, media, and worldwide joint effort, offering a guide for making a comprehensive and impartial society for ladies.

1. **Financial Strengthening Arrangements:**

Financial strengthening arrangements ought to focus on the production of a comprehensive and steady climate for ladies to partake effectively in the labor force and pioneering adventures. Key arrangement proposals include:

1. **Equal Pay and Work environment Correspondence:**
   Order and implement approaches that command equivalent compensation for equivalent work, guaranteeing that ladies get fair pay. Execute working environment balance drives that address orientation based separation, provocation, and predispositions, cultivating a culture of inclusivity.
2. **Access to Monetary Assets:**
   Create and grow monetary incorporation programs that furnish ladies with admittance to credit, capital, and monetary proficiency preparing. Support ladies drove endeavors through committed assets, awards, and special advance plans.
3. **Skill Improvement Projects:**

Fortify ability advancement programs custom-made to ladies, zeroing in on arising areas. Team up with enterprises to adjust ability improvement drives to showcase requests, improving ladies' employability and pioneering capacities.

2. Instruction Arrangements:

Training approaches ought to zero in on further developing access, quality, and inclusivity in schooling, encouraging a climate where young ladies and ladies can flourish scholastically. Key approach suggestions include:

1. **Quality Training for All:**
   Put resources into foundation, educator preparing, and educational program advancement to guarantee the conveyance of value schooling. Address differences in instructive assets among metropolitan and rustic regions, accentuating inclusivity and variety.

2. **Promotion of STEM Instruction:**
   Carry out approaches that urge young ladies to seek after STEM schooling and professions. Lay out grants, mentorship projects, and STEM-centered drives to break orientation generalizations and increment portrayal in these fields.

3. **Measures to Address Dropout Rates:**

Acquaint designated intercessions with address dropout rates among young adult young ladies, including monetary motivating forces, mindfulness missions, and local area commitment programs. Establish a strong climate that empowers young ladies to change consistently from essential to optional and advanced education.

3. Medical services Strategies:

Medical services strategies ought to focus on ladies' wellbeing and prosperity, tending to explicit difficulties they face. Key approach suggestions include:

1. **Reproductive Medical services Access:**
   Guarantee general admittance to far reaching regenerative medical care administrations, including family arranging, maternal wellbeing, and feminine cleanliness. Execute mindfulness missions to destigmatize ladies' medical problems and advance open exchange.

2. **Digital Wellbeing Drives:**
   Coordinate computerized wellbeing arrangements and telemedicine to improve admittance to medical care administrations, especially in remote and underserved regions. Influence innovation to give data, backing, and preventive medical services measures for ladies.

3. **Specialized Medical care Drives:**

Lay out specific medical services drives that address the extraordinary wellbeing challenges looked by ladies, like maternal mortality, non-transmittable illnesses, and emotional well-being. Team up with medical care experts, NGOs, and local area pioneers to execute and screen these drives.

4. Lawful Changes and Requirement Approaches:

Lawful changes and requirement approaches are critical for safeguarding ladies' freedoms and guaranteeing equity in instances of orientation based separation and viciousness. Key arrangement suggestions include:

1. **Strengthening Regulations Against Orientation Based Savagery:**
   Reinforce and uphold regulations connected with orientation based brutality, badgering, and segregation. Lay out specific courts and quick track lawful cycles for bodies of evidence including brutality against ladies, guaranteeing quick and fair equity.

2. **Legal Help Administrations Extension:**
Extend the compass of legitimate guide administrations to guarantee that ladies, particularly those from minimized networks, approach lawful help. Make mindfulness missions to teach ladies about their privileges and accessible lawful response components.

3. **Property Privileges:**

Audit and change property regulations to guarantee that ladies have equivalent privileges to property and legacy. Execute strategies that enable ladies to affirm their property privileges and safeguard them from unlawful dispossession.

5. Political Support and Portrayal Strategies:
Strategies pointed toward upgrading ladies' political investment and portrayal are fundamental for making comprehensive administration structures. Key strategy proposals include:

1. **Expanding Reservations to Higher Administrative Bodies:**
Stretch out bookings for ladies to higher administrative bodies, including state congregations and the public parliament. Advance orientation delicate discretionary cycles that urge more ladies to challenge decisions and stand firm on initiative situations.

2. **Promoting Ladies Pioneers:**
Urge ideological groups to advance and support ladies pioneers effectively. Lay out mentorship programs, authority preparing, and limit building drives to plan people for influential positions in governmental issues.

3. **Public Mindfulness Missions:**

Lead public mindfulness missions to feature the significance of ladies' voices in political navigation. Challenge generalizations and inclinations that might ruin ladies' political desires through designated media missions and local area commitment.

6. Innovation and Advanced Consideration Arrangements:
Innovation and advanced consideration approaches ought to zero in on connecting the orientation computerized separation and utilizing innovation for ladies' strengthening. Key arrangement suggestions include:

1. **Digital Education Projects:**
Carry out computerized education programs that target ladies of any age, furnishing them with the abilities expected to explore the advanced scene. Team up with instructive establishments, NGOs, and confidential area substances to guarantee far and wide admittance to advanced proficiency drives.

2. **Affordable Web Access:**
Grow drives that give reasonable web access and cell phones to ladies, particularly

in rustic and underserved regions. Cultivate public-private associations to make innovation centers and hatcheries explicitly intended for ladies business visionaries.

3. **Inclusive Innovation Approaches:**

Foster strategies that energize the formation of orientation comprehensive advancements and computerized stages. Advance the cooperation of ladies in STEM fields and tech business through designated motivations and backing programs.

7. Family and Local area Commitment Strategies:

Strategies advancing family and local area commitment are imperative for establishing a steady climate for ladies' strengthening. Key approach proposals include:

1. **Community Mindfulness Projects:**
   Carry out local area mindfulness programs that draw in families and networks in discussions about orientation correspondence, ladies' freedoms, and the advantages of ladies' strengthening. Use nearby pioneers, public venues, and social drives to work with these conversations.

2. **Men and Young men Inclusion:**
   Plan drives that include men and young men in upholding for orientation equity. Advance positive manliness and challenge hurtful orientation standards through school programs, local area occasions, and media crusades.

3. **Supportive Drives for Ladies:**

Make public venues that give data, backing, and guiding explicitly for ladies. Foster drives that commend ladies' accomplishments, cultivate mentorship valuable open doors, and make networks for expert and self-improvement.

8. Media Proficiency and Orientation Touchy Substance Approaches:

Strategies pointed toward advancing media education and orientation touchy substance are critical for molding positive cultural perspectives towards ladies. Key approach proposals include:

1. **Media Proficiency in Training:**
   Incorporate media proficiency programs into school educational plans to outfit understudies with the abilities to fundamentally examine media content. Team up with media associations and instructive organizations to foster far reaching media proficiency drives.

2. **Regulatory Structures for Capable Media:**
   Lay out administrative structures that support mindful and orientation delicate media rehearses. Implement rules that advance positive and comprehensive depictions of ladies in media content, including notices, TV programs, and news announcing.

3. Collaboration with Ladies' Promotion Gatherings:

Encourage cooperation between media associations and ladies' backing gatherings to make content that reflects different accounts and difficulties generalizations. Support drives that enhance ladies' voices in media, guaranteeing a decent portrayal.

9. Worldwide Joint effort Approaches:

Strategies for worldwide coordinated effort are fundamental for influence global assets, ability, and backing for ladies' strengthening. Key arrangement proposals include:

1. **Partnerships with Worldwide Organizations:**
   Fortify associations with worldwide associations, including the Unified Countries, NGOs, and global advancement offices, to share best practices and assets. Take part effectively in global gatherings zeroed in on ladies' privileges and orientation fairness.

2. **Engagement in Worldwide Movements:**
   Effectively participate in worldwide developments and missions that supporter for ladies' privileges. Team up with worldwide organizations to enhance the effect of ladies' strengthening drives and add to an aggregate worldwide exertion.

3. **Exchange Projects and Information Transfer:**

Work with trade programs, information move drives, and worldwide gatherings to improve cooperation and learning. Make stages for sharing effective models of ladies' strengthening that can be adjusted and carried out across various social settings.

9.3 Addressing emerging challenges and adapting to societal changes

Addressing arising difficulties and adjusting to cultural changes is fundamental for maintaining and upgrading the headway made in ladies' strengthening in India. As the financial scene develops, new obstacles and open doors emerge, requiring a dynamic and responsive methodology. In this investigation, we dive into the arising provokes and propose techniques to adjust to cultural changes, guaranteeing that the excursion towards ladies' strengthening stays strong and powerful.

1. **Mechanical Headways and Advanced Orientation Separation:**

The quick speed of innovative progressions presents the two amazing open doors and difficulties for ladies' strengthening. While innovation can be a strong empowering influence, the computerized orientation partition stays a huge concern. Ladies, particularly in provincial and minimized networks, may confront hindrances like restricted admittance to computerized framework, absence of advanced proficiency, and social limitations.

Tending to the Advanced Orientation Gap:

1. Carry out designated computerized education projects to furnish ladies with fundamental innovation abilities.
2. Grow drives that give reasonable web access and gadgets to ladies in underserved regions.
3. Encourage associations with the confidential area to make ladies agreeable innovation spaces and hatcheries.

2. Changing Nature of Work and Monetary Open doors:

The idea of work is going through changes, with a shift towards the gig economy and far off business. Ladies should be situated to use these open doors while tending to difficulties like work weakness, inconsistent compensation, and adjusting work and family obligations.

Adjusting to the Changing Work Scene:

1. Foster approaches that guarantee equivalent open doors, pay, and advantages for ladies in the gig economy.
2. Carry out adaptable work game plans and childcare backing to address balance between serious and fun activities challenges.
3. Advance business venture among ladies by giving admittance to assets, mentorship, and financing.

3. Psychological wellness and Prosperity:

Psychological wellness has earned respect as an essential part of in general prosperity. Ladies might confront extraordinary psychological wellness challenges connected with cultural assumptions, orientation based brutality, and the weight of different jobs. Addressing psychological wellness concerns is necessary to complete ladies' strengthening.

Focusing on Emotional well-being Backing:

1. Coordinate emotional wellness mindfulness and backing programs into instructive educational plans.
2. Lay out guiding administrations and helplines for ladies confronting emotional well-being difficulties.
3. Train medical care experts to perceive and address orientation explicit emotional wellness issues.

4. Natural Maintainability and Orientation:

The crossing point of orientation and natural maintainability is progressively obvious, with ladies frequently excessively impacted by environmental change and ecological corruption. In rustic regions, ladies are essential parental figures and endure the worst part of water shortage, deforestation, and rural difficulties.

Coordinating Orientation into Ecological Arrangements:

1. Consolidate an orientation delicate methodology in ecological strategies and protection drives.
2. Engage ladies in provincial regions with supportable cultivating practices and admittance to clean energy.
3. Remember people for dynamic cycles connected with natural protection and environment activity.

5. Multifacetedness and Various Characters:

Perceiving the interconnection of ladies' personalities is vital for comprehensive strengthening. Ladies from minimized networks face intensified difficulties because of their orientation, station, class, and different variables. Tending to these perplexing crossing points is fundamental for guaranteeing that strengthening endeavors are genuinely comprehensive.

Comprehensive Arrangements and Projects:

1. Execute diverse arrangements that address the extraordinary difficulties looked by ladies from underestimated networks.
2. Advance variety and portrayal in administrative roles across areas.
3. Team up with grassroots associations to comprehend and address local area explicit requirements.

6. Worldwide Pandemics and Wellbeing Emergencies:

The Coronavirus pandemic featured the weakness of ladies to wellbeing emergencies, financial shocks, and expanded aggressive behavior at home. Future wellbeing emergencies might present comparable difficulties, requiring a proactive and orientation touchy reaction.

Building Strength in Wellbeing Emergency Reaction:

1. Foster alternate courses of action that focus on ladies' wellbeing, monetary security, and wellbeing during wellbeing emergencies.
2. Reinforce social wellbeing nets to offer help for ladies confronting monetary difficulties.
3. Bring issues to light about the effect of wellbeing emergencies on ladies and guarantee their voices are heard in dynamic cycles.

7. Instruction and Abilities for What's in store:

The abilities expected for the future labor force are developing quickly, determined by progressions in innovation. Guaranteeing that ladies approach schooling and preparing in arising fields is fundamental for their support in the labor force.

Adjusting Schooling for Future Abilities:

1. Update instructive educational plans to incorporate STEM schooling and computerized proficiency since the beginning.
2. Give grants and motivations to ladies seeking after training and vocations in arising fields.
3. Encourage coordinated efforts between instructive organizations and ventures to adjust ability advancement to showcase needs.

8. Network protection and Online Security:

With expanded computerized commitment, ladies are helpless to online provocation, cyberbullying, and dangers to their security. Protecting ladies' internet based spaces and guaranteeing their advanced security is fundamental to their strengthening.

Advancing Network safety Mindfulness:

1. Lead network protection mindfulness crusades focusing on ladies, everything being equal.
2. Lay out systems for revealing web-based provocation and offering help to casualties.
3. Team up with web access suppliers and virtual entertainment stages to establish more secure internet based conditions for ladies.

9. Maturing Populace and Older Ladies:

As India's populace ages, the prosperity of older ladies turns into a basic concern. More established ladies might confront difficulties connected with wellbeing, monetary security, and cultural mentalities.

Supporting Old Ladies:

1. Execute social government assistance programs that take care of the particular necessities of older ladies.
2. Make people group based emotionally supportive networks and sporting open doors for old ladies.
3. Advocate for strategies that safeguard the privileges and pride of old ladies, including legacy freedoms.

10. Media and Portrayal:

Media assumes a strong part in forming cultural discernments. Guaranteeing that media portrayal is comprehensive and liberated from generalizations is essential for encouraging inspirational perspectives towards ladies.

Advancing Comprehensive Media Representation:

1. Advocate for orientation touchy media content through administrative structures.
2. Urge media associations to depict assorted accounts and positive good examples for ladies.
3. Support drives that enhance the voices of ladies in media, including news coverage and filmmaking.